WRITERS AND THEIR W[...]

ISOBEL ARMSTRONG
General [...]

D0420805

[...]E UNI[...]
[...]

FLEUR ADCOCK

FLEUR ADCOCK

Janet Wilson

NORTHCOTE

BRITISH
COUNCIL

For Jack

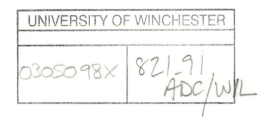
© Copyright 2007 by Janet Wilson
First published in 2007 by Northcote House Publishers Ltd,
Horndon, Tavistock, Devon, PL19 9NQ, United Kingdom.
Tel: +44 (0) 1822 810066 Fax: +44 (0) 1822 810034.

British Library Cataloguing-in-Publication Data
A catalogue record for this book is available from the British Library

ISBN 978-0-7463-1035-9 hardcover
ISBN 978-0-7463-1040-3 paperback

Typeset by PDQ Typesetting, Newcastle-under-Lyme
Printed and bound in the United Kingdom

Contents

Acknowledgements

The author and the publishers gratefully acknowledge Fleur Adcock for permission to reprint poems from *The Eye of the Hurricane* and Bloodaxe Books to quote from *Poems 1960-2000* by Fleur Adcock.

Biographical Outline

1934   Born on 10 February as Kareen Fleur Adcock in
            Papakura, New Zealand near Drury where both sets
            of grandparents lived; father working as school
            teacher at Graham's Beach (on the Manakau Har-
            bour).

1935   10 November: Birth of sister Marilyn (later Marilyn
            Duckworth); family living at Kuaotunu (in the
            Coromandel Peninsula).

1937–38   Family living in Palmerston North where Adcock
            attends kindergarten.

1938   August to December: Family move to Rangiwahia.

1939   Adcock attends Tokorangi School for one term.
            Family lives in school shelter shed. May: father leaves
            for England to study for a PhD in psychology at
            Birkbeck College, University of London. 23 June: rest
            of family leaves. Adcock attends eleven different
            schools in the next seven-and-a-half years.

1939–40   Family settles in Wincham Avenue, Sidcup where
            Adcock's father works in Lamorbey Civil Defence
            Depot, Sidcup, and her mother in the Ambulance
            Service. Adcock attends Halfway Street School, then
            St Gertrude's Convent, Hatherley Road.

1940–41   Adcock and Marilyn evacuated during the Blitz to
            Grange Farm, Scalford near Melton Mowbray in
            Leicestershire to stay with relatives; attends Scalford
            School. Begins writing poetry.

1941   February to mid-September: family reunited in
            Surrey, first in Honeycrock Lane, Salfords, Adcock
            attending Salfords School, then in 'Top Lodge',

	Outwood, attending Outwood School. October: family now living in Woodside Way, Salfords; Adcock attending St John's School, Redhill.
1944	27 June to 3 August: sisters evacuated again to Grange Farm and attend Scalford School; then to Hawthorn, Corsham, Wiltshire, where they board with families. Both attend Neston School, then Adcock leaves for Chippenham Secondary School having passed the 11-plus at Redhill. November, sisters live with mother in Chippenham.
1945	Living in Frant and attending schools in Tunbridge Wells.
1945–7	May: family reunited at 28 Hatherley Road, Sidcup where Mr Adcock is regional organizer for the WEA (Workers' Educational Association). Adcock attends Chislehurst and Sidcup County Grammar School for Girls.
1947	15 March: family sail for New Zealand after Mr Adcock is appointed as a junior lecturer at Victoria University of Wellington. After a reunion with grandparents in Drury and Papatoetoe, family move to Wellington where Adcock attends Wellington Girls' College.
1951–5	Attends Victoria University of Wellington where she studies Classics. Completes an MA with First Class honours.
1952	Marries poet Alistair Campbell, whose *Mine Eyes Dazzle* was published in 1950. Adcock becomes friendly with James K. Baxter. Her first poem published in *Salient*, the student newspaper of Victoria University of Wellington.
1954	Birth of son Gregory.
1957	Birth of son Andrew.
1957	Separation from Alistair Campbell and agreement that Gregory should stay with him.
1958	Moves to Dunedin with Andrew to become junior lecturer in Classics at the University of Otago.
1959	Works in University of Otago library while training for British library qualification by correspondence. Becomes friendly with other writers including

Charles Brasch, editor of the literary quarterly, *Land-fall*, who subsequently publishes several of her poems.

1962   Marries briefly the writer Barry Crump, known for his novels and sketches of life as a deer-culler; moves to Wellington and works in the Turnbull Library.

1963   January: Adcock returns to England with Andrew, and after a temporary job at a polytechnic, is employed as a librarian at the Colonial Office (later, following the merger of government departments, incorporated into the Foreign and Commonwealth Office library), and settles in East Finchley where she still lives. Begins to attend London meetings of Edward Lucie-Smith's Group.

1964   Publication in New Zealand of *The Eye of the Hurricane* (A.H. & A.W. Reed)

1967   Publication by Oxford University Press (OUP) in England of *Tigers* incorporating some poems from *The Eye of the Hurricane*

1971   Publication of *High Tide in the Garden* (OUP).

1974   Publication of *The Scenic Route* (OUP).

1975–6   November to February: first return trip to New Zealand for thirteen years.

1977–8   September to June: holds Arts Council Creative Writing Fellowship at the Charlotte Mason College of Education in Ambleside.

1979   Resigns from the Foreign and Commonwealth Office Library to become a full-time writer. Publication of *The Inner Harbour* (OUP) and *Below Loughrigg* (Blood-axe).

1979-81   Northern Arts Literary Fellow at universities of Newcastle and Durham.

1982   Publication of her edition of *The Oxford Book of Contemporary New Zealand Poetry* (OUP). Changes her name by deed poll to Fleur Adcock, always her professional name, omitting Kareen.

1983   Publication of *Selected Poems* (OUP) which won the New Zealand Book Award for Poetry in 1984; and a book of translations, *The Virgin and the Nightingale: Medieval Latin Lyrics* (Bloodaxe).

1984	April to June: Literary Fellow at the University of East Anglia. Visits Romania for the British Council and begins learning Romanian. Made Fellow of the Royal Society of Literature.
1986	Attends Adelaide Festival. Briefly Writer in Residence at the University of Adelaide. Publication of *Hotspur: a ballad for music* (Bloodaxe) and *The Incident Book* (OUP).
1987	5 June: Death of father. Publication of her edition of *The Faber Book of Twentieth Century Women's Poetry*. Second visit to Romania for the British Council.
1988	Publication of *Meeting the Comet* (Bloodaxe).
1989	Publishes translations of poems by Grete Tartler, *Orient Express* (OUP).
1990	Third visit to Romania for the British Council.
1991	Publication of *Time-Zones* (OUP), and translations of poems by Daniela Crasnaru, *Letters from Darkness* (OUP).
1994	Publication of an edition of *Hugh Primas and the Archpoet* (Cambridge University Press).
1995	Publication of *The Oxford Book of Creatures*, co-edited with Jacqueline Simms (OUP).
1996	Awarded an OBE for her contribution to New Zealand literature.
1997	Publication of *Looking Back* (OUP).
2000	Publication of *Poems: 1966–2000* (Bloodaxe) following closure of Oxford University Press modern poetry list.
2001	31 July: Death of mother.
2006	7 June: Awarded the Queen's Gold Medal for Poetry. 11 December: awarded honorary doctorate by Victoria University of Wellington, New Zealand.

Abbreviations and References

A.   Appendix to *Fleur Adcock*, 127–33.
B.   'Beginnings', *Islands* 26 (1979): 347–56.
BS   'Bluebell Seasons', *Cherries on a Plate: New Zealand Writers Talk about their Sisters*, ed. Marilyn Duckworth (Auckland: Random House, 1996), 220–45.
LOW   'A Lifetime of Writing', *Beyond Expectations, Fourteen New Zealand Women Write about their Lives*, ed. Margaret Clark (Wellington: Allen & Unwin/Port Nicholson Press, 1986), 99–112.
OUP   Oxford University Press.
Poems   *Poems: 1960-2000* (Newcastle: Bloodaxe, 2000).
RB   'Rural Blitz: Fleur Adcock's English Childhood', *Poetry Review* 74:2 (June, 1984): 5–12.
TEOH   *The Eye of the Hurricane* (Wellington and Auckland: A.H. and A.W. Reed, 1963). (Poems from this volume which have not been reprinted and are referred to in this study are included in the Appendix).
TLS   *Times Literary Supplement*.
TWIH   'The Way it Happens', *The Poet's Voice and Craft*, ed. C.B. McCully (Manchester: Carcanet Press, 1994), 147–65.

1

Introduction:
A Double Displacement

In January 1963 Fleur Adcock arrived in London from New Zealand with her five-year-old son, Andrew. She had few prospects: a handful of poems published in literary journals in New Zealand, the possibility of a published volume, a qualification in librarianship, and a determination to make her name as a poet. In the depths of winter she found employment as a librarian, first in a polytechnic and then in the Colonial Office (later incorporated into the Foreign and Commonwealth Office). After some moving around she found and eventually bought a house in East Finchley where she settled and lives today. Within a decade she had become known as one of Britain's foremost women poets, a reputation which she has sustained ever since.[1]

This was not, in fact, Adcock's first visit to England, but a willed return. In 1939, at the age of five, she and her younger sister Marilyn had been taken by their parents to the UK where her father had enrolled for a PhD in Psychology at Birkbeck College, University of London. Seven-and-a-half formative years were spent in the south of England during the war before the family returned to New Zealand in 1947. During this time Adcock came to think of herself as English. Departure was a shock which led her thirteen-year-old self to romanticize England as the place of her dreams, the source of her most intense feelings and passions; this perception of England as 'home' coincided with a growing psychological estrangement from New Zealand over the next sixteen years there.

1963, therefore, defines a turning point for the twenty-nine-year-old Adcock, who by then recognized that poetry was the

1

guiding influence in her life. Verse published subsequently is marked by the consequences of her decision to live outside New Zealand, but also to live as an outsider in England. England offered her greater opportunities but her separation from family and loved ones in New Zealand came to be experienced as a conflict of loyalties. She said in 1993: 'everything to do with here [Britain] and New Zealand is insoluble. My life is full of these irreconcilable things.'[2] However the expanded horizons apparent in all her work published since 1964 suggest that the freedoms of expatriation enabled her to establish a sense of 'belonging' in her poetry. She writes: 'I feed on solitude, when I can find it. I read. I listen. I walk about looking at the world. The happiest state is to have just begun writing the next poem'.[3] Her exploration of these contradictory feelings – ambivalence about New Zealand, nostalgia about England as the 'imaginary homeland' – map a distinctive trajectory.

In the last forty years Adcock's poetry has been acknowledged as contributing to the different fashions of the post-war British literary tradition: her concise expression and meticulous craftsmanship were seen as meshing with the aesthetic values of the Group (the poetry circle founded by Philip Hobsbaum); her penchant for the strange and surreal and for de-familiarizing linguistic innovation aligned her with the Martian poets, such as Craig Raine and Christopher Reid, in the 1970s; her preoccupation with women's issues made her prominent in the 1980s. The personal journey, however, can be traced from her earliest 'placeless' poems which anticipate her rejection of New Zealand; in the multi-locational attachments formed through travel to Europe, the Orient and Northern Ireland in her first decade in England; in the plural subjectivities emerging from the 'to and fro' pattern of her life established upon her first return to New Zealand in 1975; in the spiritual 'discovery' of the landscape of the Lake District and the north of England in the late 1970s; in the broadening social and political references stemming from engagement with the women's movement during the Thatcherite eighties; in the discovery of interzonal temporalities and spaces coinciding with her genealogical research on her British ancestors in the 1990s; and in the renewed exploration of her childhood in both countries in poems written since 2000. Not just in thirteen volumes of verse but also in autobiographical writing – letters, diaries and family history – Adcock has obsessively traced her multiple psychological and physical journeys, recently returning to her earliest memories in New Zealand.

This study examines Adcock's trajectory through the frameworks of migration and diaspora. Diaspora is a term derived from the Greek *diasperien* (*dia*- across, and *sperien*- to sow or scatter seeds) and has connotations of dissemination and dispersion. It traditionally refers to mass migration or exile, but in the late twentieth century 'conceptualisation of exilic or nostalgic displacement' from the native homeland has acquired 'new epistemological, political and identitarian resonances' as the categories of home and belonging have been destabilized and new reference points established.[4] Diaspora theory stresses the rupture of departure and loss experienced by the diasporic subject, arguing that the 'diasporic imaginary' creates an imaginary, fantasized homeland as compensation.[5] Yet 'desire for a homeland' is not the same as a 'homing desire' and diaspora, with its enforced reassessment of origins, 'creates the desire to reinvent and to rewrite home as much as a desire to come to terms with an exile from it'.[6] Diasporic writing is situated between the margins and the mainstream and encompasses the cross-cultural experiences of migrant writers for whom the distinction between being inside and outside a culture loses definition, who acquire hyphenated identities and live hybrid lives.[7] As Adcock's poems in *Time-Zones* show, living diasporically creates awareness of 'in-between zones' where identity can be constructed and deconstructed, enabling a critical repositioning of nostalgia for home within a discourse of arrival and relocation and a possession of dispossession.

Adcock's migration in 1963 is part of an historic movement which led to the questioning of assumptions of British identity: the exodus in the 1950s and 1960s to the imperial centre of colonial artists and writers: Australians – Peter Porter, Clive James, Barry Humphries, and Germaine Greer; New Zealanders – Janet Frame, Kevin Ireland, Dan Davin, James Courage and Hubert Witheford; and the Windrush generation of Caribbean migrant writers – Sam Selvon, George Lamming, the West Indian, V.S. Naipaul and later Salman Rushdie. Their writing about exile, alienation and dispossession from an outsider's position has helped to reshape concepts of Britishness. Adcock's earliest perceptions of translocation are subjective, defining unexpected shifts in her self-image in ways reminiscent of the surreal distortions found in her poetry. Her arrival in 1963 began to reshape her idea of 'belonging' by demanding an awareness of national identity:

> I had never intended to be a New Zealander, and it was not until I was back in England that I found I had become one. I experienced culture shock for the second time in my life, but now it was accompanied by excitement and a sense of the world opening out instead of closing in.[8]

Adcock's unusual circumstances define a paradigm whose duality and reversal of points of origin and identification differentiate her from the familiar diasporic subject who nostalgically longs to return to the imaginary homeland of their birth. Already a divided subject because of her double displacement as a child, her origins, both familial and genealogical, have demanded extensive interrogation. In her personal mythology New Zealand, the place of her birth, represented a state of exile: its location as the true home came to be superseded in her 'diasporic imaginary' by England. As a first generation New Zealander on her father's side, she saw England as a more 'authentic' point of origin, while New Zealand's history of colonial migration constituted, essentially, a break in the continuity of the European past.

This study traces the developing reference points and identifications in Adcock's verse that become constitutive of her hybrid identity as a New Zealand-born poet, now living and working in England, who thinks of herself as English. It also explores how nostalgia for an archaic idea of home, the search for origins, the trauma of return, dual nationalities and divided loyalties, reflect other discontinuities such as the divided subject's fractured and fragmentary ego. Geographical displacement might, then, be read as a synecdoche of psychological dislocation.[9] The image of the split consciousness appears in many early poems where Adcock deliberately loses control, producing disorienting shifts between different states such as consciousness, dreaming, the unconscious and nightmare. Other poems about male-female relationships reveal self-

4

dislocation as a blurring of the boundaries between the self and the other. Finally, the relationship between her gender and doubly displaced status as an expatriate writer grappling with the fraught question of nationality, is examined as a central, complex one.

Adcock's handling of disorientation can be related to Stuart Hall's view that 'cultural identity is not an essence but a position':[10] this perception is central to her deconstructive, ludic postmodernism, and informs her play with poetic form and her linguistic inventiveness. Adcock's growing command of multiple fields of signification enables her to redeploy earlier images of disorientation into new configurations of cultural syncretism.[11] This might constitute a dialogic, reconciliatory structure, a deconstruction of fictive identities or a redrawing of the boundaries between different categories or species; but in each case she exposes the cultural manufacture of identity, even bidding farewell to the biological structure of all species in 'Last Song'. A writer who locates herself between the margins of the nation and the changing mainstream, occupying 'interstitial' ground, Adcock reconfigures conventions of 'home' by becoming accountable to more than one location, tradition and concept of origins. She transgresses those borders which divide nations and hemispheres, people, spaces, and temporalities in order to locate herself in more than one place at any one time. In writing about her ancestors, 'home' is once more redefined, as the boundaries between life and death are dissolved in order to reconnect with her buried forebears.

Such subterranean shifts in Adcock's later work, indicative of attempts to reconcile or relativize dichotomous oppositions, are effected through poetic experimentation, mastery of technique, and a 'flexible, all-purpose style, to allow herself the widest possible range of response'.[12] Yet her conversational tone masking sharp critique, her clarity and accessibility skewed by disorientation or ludic wit, her balanced composure mastering tension and duress are manifestations of complex adjustments to an identity as essentially an English 'outsider' writer as much as a bifurcated New Zealand-English one. These shifts are displayed throughout her œuvre in psychologically intense poetry which challenges received notions of the ordinary and unsettles social values and assumptions. In making displacement and dispossession – what Homi Bhabha calls the 'middle passage' of contemporary culture – her own territory, in privileging those little known spaces between the normal and the unfamiliar, and in recontextualising her own transitions of identity within diaspora, Adcock might be seen as a voice for our age.[13]

Like other postcolonial writers of the ex-British empire, such as the Windrush generation of the early 1960s, Adcock can be differentiated from expatriate modernists like Scott Fitzgerald, Auden, Hemingway, Eliot and Pound who moved from one metropolitan centre to another. She also contrasts with colonial modernists such as James Joyce and New Zealand's most famous expatriate writer, Katherine Mansfield, whose exile created the desire to impose order on a mobile world and who found stasis by turning to the original homeland and minutely recording its features.[14] Adcock's decision to examine her discontent with New Zealand from an English distance and to explore her English ancestral heritage, sets her apart, although the growth of her ironic awareness in exile and the triggering of memory to recreate images of her earliest childhood show some overlap with the Joyce of *The Portrait of the Artist as a Young Man*.

Although the experience of migration and exile was less extreme for Adcock than for colonial migrants of different ethnicities, her exploration of exile and expatriation suggests affinities with metropolitan-based writers like V.S. Naipaul, Sam Selvon, George Lamming, and more recently, Andrea Levy and Monica Ali. They have all mapped, in their alienation, a search for both home and identity. Adcock's double displacement evokes comparisons with many Caribbean writers who are born into a world of exile: indeed, this form of dispossession may go some way to explain the sense of detachment in her work. But her nostalgic idealization of England and her English childhood which led her to back-migrate and to search for her ancestors, contrast radically with the situation of the Black Atlantic and its triangulated geography which meant, for many Caribbeans, that migration to Britain was never profoundly a homecoming.

This study reads Adcock's work from the perspective of the life story. In doing so it aims to revise her reputation as a mainstream poet, in tune with the changing literary and aesthetic fashions of post-war British poetry, by aligning her voice with that of other migrant writers whose similar transnational, transcultural journeys to the metropolitan centre have involved an encounter with the self requiring multiple points of self-redefinition.[15] If the categories of 'race' and 'ethnicity' applied to writers of Black and Asian origin are extended to white settlers from colonies like New Zealand and Australia, then Adcock's work can be seen as inhabiting both the margins and the mainstream. The diverse perspectives offered by her diasporic habitation, her divided nationality, the dislocations of gender, all underpinning her satiric topicality, her de-familiarizing of the familiar and her curiosity about the unknown or hidden – aging, disability, ancestors – can be mapped along a spectrum ranging from margins to centre. She has recently been included in the current re-examination of British culture which Asian and Black British voices have generated.[16] Yet Adcock's interrogation of her identity also involves a questioning of her current location, and an outsider's scrutiny of the English. Like Linton Kwesi Johnson or Grace Nicholls, her work can be seen as redefining ideas of Britishness and contributing to the mapping of multicultural Britain along the lines of ethnicity, gender and culture. This revisionism has increased over the last twenty years because of the impact of voices from the margins; Adcock as a mainstream poet who sustains a playful questioning of the norms of Britishness yet continues to search for her English ancestral origins contributes vitally to these discourses.

2

Early Influences: Two Hemispheres and the Divided Self

BEGINNINGS: TWO HEMISPHERES

In her earliest autobiographical account Fleur Adcock announces the central fact of her life, her divided nationality. Like most white settlers this stems from having one parent or grandparent born in Britain and another born in the colony but of British origin:

> I have spent more than half of my life in England and am not sure whether I can now be called a New Zealander, but I was born one. My mother and her mother were also New Zealand-born, of Ulster stock, but my father was English and had arrived with his parents at the age of ten to settle in wild country near Pirongia. (B. 347)

In acknowledging this mixed ancestry, Adcock 'naturalises' her decision to repatriate, to return to the country of her father's birth, as though the right of someone who can claim dual English and Irish ancestry. This personal mythology points to the psychological impasse of the white settler (or the white Creole, the white settler's descendant) of the Second World, who according to Alan Lawson is:

> ...caught between two First Worlds, two origins of authority and authenticity, the originating world of Europe, the imperium, as source of the Second World's principle cultural authority; and that other First World, that of the First Nations, whose authority the settlers not only effaced and replaced but also desired.[1]

The white settler suffers from separation from Europe and an 'anxiety of proximity' in relation to the indigene. Ambivalence towards the Maori, New Zealand's indigenous people, never featured strongly in Adcock's complex self-identification, although her recent genealogical research embodies another characteristic of the white settler, the desire to reconnect to pure and authentic origins. At the age of eighteen she married the half-Polynesian poet, Alistair Te Ariki Campbell, who was born in the Cook Islands and brought up in Rarotonga. Campbell's first volume, *Mine Eyes Dazzle* (1950), had been an instant success. Theirs was a whirlwind courtship.[2] Like that of the poet James K. Baxter and his Maori wife, Jackie C. Sturm, later a published writer herself, their inter-racial marriage reflected the egalitarian myth which prevailed in New Zealand at a time when government policy on race relations was one of assimilation.[3] Campbell's early reputation as a poet owed nothing to his Polynesian origins; he was known primarily as a significant Wellington regional poet until the late 1970s when he began to reclaim his ethnicity and kinship in the volume *The Dark Lord of Savaiki* (1980).[4] This shift coincided with the renaissance of Maori writing, increasing ethnic politicization principally over land rights, the formation of the Waitangi Tribunal to arbitrate on reparations of land and fishing rights, and the transformation of New Zealand/Aotearoa into a bicultural society through national policies, such as the teaching of the Maori language in schools and wānanga (Maori teaching institutions and universities).

By contrast, Adcock was deeply troubled by feelings of displacement from England, where she spent formative childhood years from 1939 to 1947, and she embarked on a profound interrogation of her own beginnings and her family's origins. It emerges in poems about her early life in Drury with her grandparents and parents, such as 'The Water Below' and 'Script', poems rejecting New Zealand like 'Ngauranga Gorge Hill', poems about settler life like 'Settlers', and most fully in the ancestral poems of *Looking Back* (1997), in which she recreates the voices of her forebears, establishing a dialogue with the past. Such acts of recreation have defined and consolidated her doubly displaced, yet relocated position. Adcock's preoccupation with genealogy might be an antidote to the ruptures and discontinuities that her long separation from New Zealand has provoked, or even a finale, since 'Goodbye', the final poem in *Poems 1960–2000*, has been read as a farewell to her art.[5] But recent poems about her earliest memories, like 'Kuaotunu' and 'Linseed', show the continued attachment to her place of birth as important to her mature British-based identity.[6] The cultural polarization of the labels, 'New Zealander' and 'English', belie the complex psychological and emotional readjustments which expatriation has demanded. Her poetry, proof of this encounter, also attests its resistance to closure.

Although Adcock moves easily between fantasy, the surreal and the real in verse, in her autobiographical writings, faithful to facts, always aware of the instabilities of memory, she attempts to ascertain the truth in the broadest sense possible. She has said: 'I wouldn't embroider facts. I believe in the absolute, direct, pure truth'.[7] Her earliest memories establish how her relationships with her sister, parents and relatives created the context in which she first began to write poetry. Born in February 1934 in a nursing home in Papakura, an outlying suburb of Auckland, and followed eighteen months later by a sister, Marilyn, Adcock spent her early life in small country towns in the North Island – Graham's Beach, Kuaotunu, Rangiwahia, Tokorangi, Palmerston North – for her father, a school teacher, moved from one 'tiny backblocks school to another' (B. 347). The family base was in Drury, where her mother's family had lived since the 1870s, running the village store and farming, where several great-uncles lived and where her father's family had settled. In 'Going Back' – written on her first trip back to New Zealand in the mid-1970s – the child's struggle with spelling names and finding locations is foregrounded: 'There were always places I couldn't spell or couldn't find on maps – / too small but swollen in family legend' (*Poems*, 113). Likewise her random images: 'a wall with blackboards; a gate where I swung, the wind bleak in the telegraph wires', contrast to family anchorage – 'Mother in this or that school house kitchen/ singing' – and 'familiar bases;/ Drury again, Christmas Days in grandparents' houses.' The fragmented nature of these memories and the child's imperfect grasp image the insignificance of these places to the returned narrator. Adcock listened to her mother reading nursery rhymes, songs and verses, some about her daughters: 'Who's that knocking at the garden gate? / Little Fleur and Marilyn with cherries on a plate'.[8] She read poetry herself when she started school at Tokorangi, and after the family moved to England, at the age of six she began writing it. This introduced a period of joy, which she looks back upon as one of the happiest in her life.

ENGLAND: 1939–1947

The family's departure from New Zealand in 1939, so that her father could study for a PhD in Psychology at Birkbeck College, London, clashed with the outbreak of war (LOW, 100). Adcock's parents, Irene and John, settled in Sidcup on the outskirts of London, and joined the Civil Defence Ambulance Service, arranging a minder for the children. Adcock later enrolled at school. Within a year the sisters were evacuated, at first to the village of Scalford, near Melton Mowbray in Leicestershire, to stay with Adcock relations, Eva and George Carter. Although they lived there for only nine months, Grange Farm 'delightfully primitive' with its animals, milking shed, barn, orchard, gas-light and candles, remained in their imaginations as a 'bubble of bliss' (RB, 6). The proximity between adult, child and animal worlds, dramatized by word play on the different connotations of 'tongue', informs 'Tongue Sandwiches', a poem about market-day lunch in the 'King's Head Hottle' (sic) in Melton. Adcock's childish curiosity, her desire for knowledge, her attempt to 'sound' English – 'syphoning up Midlands vowels/ to smother my colonial whine' – combined with a passion for reading ('tasting/ the thrilling syllables: "veterinary /surgeon", "papyrus", "manuscript"') enacts this intimacy. Harmony and rootedness in country life are projected through the adult narrator's voice which speaks with the child's voice and confirms her enthusiastic point of view:

> On the way back to Uncle's cart
> (how neat that his name was George Carter!)
> we passed the beasts in the cattle-stalls—
> their drooling lips, their slathering tongues.

> (*Poems*, 257)

11

Adcock mediates this joyful sojourn in 'In Focus', written in the late 1970s, with her responses to the death of her aunt and uncle. An unexpected flashback as she wakes up returns her to a patch of earth in the backyard, near the sheds, privy and pump:

> Inside my closed eyelids, printed out
> from some dying braincell as I awakened,
> was this close-up of granular earthy dust,
> fragments of chaff and grit, a triangular
> splinter of glass, a rusty metal washer
> on rough concrete under a wooden step.

(Poems, 95)

The cinematic frame of herself at seven at Grange Farm, 'kneeling outside the shed', opens out like a camera rolling, capturing the past as her mind relaxes the focus of the lens:

> ...let the whole scene open out
> to the pump and separator under the porch,
> the strolling chickens, the pear trees next to the yard,
> the barn full of white cats, the loaded haycart,
> the spinney...I saw it rolling on and on.

The poem recalls a return visit made after more than twenty years. Her aunt and uncle have retired, the farm has been sold, and her aunt is senile: ' "not well," / said Uncle George – little and gnarled himself – / "You'll find she doesn't talk." ' With Adcock they visit Grange Farm, now 'small, bleak and surrounded by mud'. With the stark realization, 'Both dead now', the poem becomes her answer to the finality of death. The metaphorical connotations of 'focus', 'scene' and 'rolling on' transform into 'the gradual running down of a film' as Adcock appropriates image-making in celluloid to imagine dying. She offers her aunt and uncle posthumously what she had discovered at Grange Farm in childhood, a hope:

> that for those two an after-image glowed
> in death of something better than mud and silence
> or than my minute study of a patch of ground;

(Poems, 96)

The conclusion's nostalgic recall of 'sunny ploughland, pastures, the scented orchard' replaces the mud-surrounded farmhouse of her final visit. Memories of the 'bubble of bliss' challenge death's erasure as the final line echoes and reflects the

12

transformative movement of the poem's opening focus on 'dust, chaff and grit', to the opening out of the mind's images in stanza two. This mediation of a pastoral, utopian memory by introducing a performative gesture to concretize emotions of nostalgia, longing and loss, is a characteristic of other weighty conclusions. In 'Invocation for Gregory' she deputizes to the wind 'my care' for her first born (*TEOH*, 7; A.127), in 'Please Identify Yourself' she symbolically embraces her mother's ancestors (*Poems*, 61), and 'My Father' concludes with her vow to overcome his death by finding his forebears (*Poems*, 194).

Adcock began writing poetry with a pastoral romantic flavour at Grange Farm. These early efforts contained woods, trees and wildflowers and were peopled by fairies and princesses (RB, 9; LOW, 101). Separated from their parents for nine months, the sisters wrote joint letters which included stories and drawings: the conclusion of 'Tongue Sandwiches' confirms that early on, writing was a spontaneously affectionate gesture:

> As for me, when I sat for hours
> writing a story for Mummy and Daddy,
> and folded the pages down the middle
> to make a book, I had no ambition.

> (*Poems*, 258)

When the family was reunited nine months later in 1941, living in a small gate-house on a country estate in Outwood, Surrey, Adcock was writing regularly during breaks at school. These poems, including some written in Leicestershire, became her first collection, 'published' in a notebook with the calendars for 1941–2 printed on the inside of the covers. By the age of nine she had filled another notebook with illustrated poems, ballads and songs. Writing was also a tremulous response to new experiences which would eventually separate her from family relationships. 'Outwood' records her earliest awakening to love as fairies and verdant spring flowers combine with solitary writing. Peter, who shared his hymnbook with her, inspires this 'first love poem' (RB, 6–7). Assonance and rhyme link these activities:

> 'Little fairies dancing,' I wrote,
> and 'Peter and I, we watch the birds fly,
> high in the sky, in the evening.'

> (*Poems*, 168)

13

A glimpse of snatched adult passions follows as the poem switches to Doris who took the sisters walking with a soldier: 'through the damp ferns in the wood/ into a clearing like a garden'. For Doris, love is a different form of enchantment: 'he leaned over her pink blouse/and their voices went soft and round, like petals.' (*Poems*, 169)

In 1941 the family moved to Woodside Way between Salfords and Earlswood, near the main London to Brighton Road. During the next three years the sisters mixed more with neighbouring children, encountering the world outside the family circle. Adcock founded a society called 'Secret Exploring Indians', explored Earlswood Common – 'wildish heath clumped with bracken and little copses' – and became 'addicted to English woods' with their trees, wild flowers, marshy open spaces, undergrowth for making dens, birds, squirrels, caterpillars and frogs (LOW, 102). But these scenes of pastoral discovery are juxtaposed to apparitions born of childish fantasy and fear. One of her most powerful archetypes, the male predator, can be traced to 'that night I was ten' on Earlswood Common, and the menacing spectre of 'Bogyman' who 'stands in my path':

> He is not as I had remembered him,
> though he still wears the broad-brimmed hat,
> the rubber-soled shoes and the woollen gloves.
> No face: and that soft mooning voice
> still spinning its endless distracting yarn.

> (*Poems*, 35)

This sinister figure anticipates all those nameless batterers and stalkers of her verse, most graphically realized in the monstrous-grotesque ancestor of 'A Haunting' (*Poems*, 243). In 'Bogyman' the children's imagining of '"murderers"' or '"lunatics escaped from Earlswood"' becomes the adult's experience of the

> slummocking figure in a dark
> alley, or the lover turned suddenly
> icy-faced; fingers at my throat

Finally, he is 'deconstructed', becoming 'the risk I would not take' as the narrator's mixed fascination and repugnance makes her discover similarities to her 'victimiser'. Like Bogy she is also subject to the aging process. Asking, 'what, Bogyman, shall I be at, twice my age?', she concludes: 'Or / (and now I look for the

first time / straight at you) something like you, Bogyman?'
(*Poems*, 36)

Other poems record the harsh realities of war, stressing that
nations and cultures differ, and the inexorability of fate: in
'Scalford School' France is perceived as a foreign place 'where
things were wrong in 1940', leading to the recognition of their
own national 'difference':

> But we were foreign too, of course,
> my sister and I, in spite of our
> unthinkingly acquired Leicestershire accents.

> (*Poems*, 167)

'On the School Bus' details childish savagery towards two little
girls whose mother was killed in a fatal road accident: 'the
ambulance men had had to scrape her / off the road, said the
sickening whispers'. They are offered 'a homeopathic dose of
torture /...we pulled their hair, like all the others.' (*Poems*, 169)

Revelations of class differences appear in poems written
about 1944, just after Adcock had sat the 11-plus, when the
Doodlebugs arrived. Initially enjoying refuge in a Morrison
shelter – 'cocoa and toast inside the Table Shelter, / our iron-
panelled bunker, our new den' – and under the playground at
school: 'damp tunnels / where you sang "Ten Green Bottles"
yet again / and might as well have been doing decimals'
('Earlswood', *Poems*, 169), the sisters were soon sent to Haw-
thorn, a village near Corsham in Wiltshire. Here, staying in a
two-roomed cottage, carrying water in buckets from the village
tap, finding lice in their hair and sores on their feet, they
encountered the irregularities of working-class life. 'Chippen-
ham' recreates the scenario caused by the woman they boarded
with, who kept Adcock at home for company by resetting the
clock, so causing her to miss the bus to school (LOW, 103).
'"What do you think you're playing at?"' the maths master
shouted, for her erratic attendance. And a male prefect pointed
out her bad feet: 'I felt my impetigo scabs / blaze through my
shoes. How did he know?' (*Poems*, 171–72).

In 1945 Mr Adcock began work as Kent regional organizer for
the Workers' Educational Association (WEA) while completing
his thesis, and the family was reunited once more in Sidcup,
where their English stay had begun. Their newly-purchased,

three-storey home had a cellar and stables and 'a large and satisfactorily wild garden full of fruit trees and rambling roses, with a space at the end where we kept four brown ducks' (LOW, 103). Adcock attended Chislehurst and Sidcup County Grammar School for Girls, making new friends, undertaking long bicycle rides, keeping caterpillars, and sketching in a nature notebook. There was also escapism involving plots, characters and telling stories. She and Marilyn in Brontë-esque fashion, invented a fantasy world called 'Dreamland' centring on a boarding school with a circle of imaginary friends whose tricks, escapades and games far exceeded in daring those they read about in school stories (LOW, 101; BS, 232). In real life escape was a form of defiance; at school she climbed the branches of an elm during the lunchtime:

> There was a tree higher than clouds or lighting,
> higher than any plane could fly.

> England huddled under its roots; leaves from it
> fluttered on Europe out of the sky.

> ('The High Tree', *Poems*, 173).

The panoramic vista in which both England and Europe are visible, giving:

> ...someone solitary and shy

> who liked gazing out over miles of history,
> watching it happen, like a spy

an equally expanded temporal vision, symbolically broadens the intimate domestic horizons of these years. This triumphantly rebellious gesture (at having to attend her twelfth school), which is also one of freedom, suggests the singular path Adcock will carve out, the solitariness of the occupation and the bird's eye view by which she will learn to link nations and identify cultural differences.

For a child who spent hours alone, scribbling was always a solitary act. But Adcock's earliest impulses to write also stem from belonging to a close-knit family and wishing to sustain intimacy with her parents when she and Marilyn were separated from them. Her dependence on the written word for communication with those close to her, Adcock claims, gave her the 'lifelong habit of writing' (LOW, 101); it also explains her affection for the verse epistle. Other urges such as the desire to play, show off, enjoy make believe, invent games, and explore the creative possibilities of language contributed. Yet the private creation of meaning through writing did not mean abandoning the family circle for long. A self-declared romantic, Adcock's imaginative responses to her surroundings were nurtured in these early years. Her models were her mother Irene's verse, and the poems Irene read to her – nursery rhymes and Georgian verse such as Rupert Brooke's 'Those I Have Loved' or Harold Monroe's 'Overheard on a Saltmarsh' with its refrain 'Nymph, nymph, what are your beads? / Green glass, goblin...'. But these pastoral, idyllic beginnings have a darker side, reflecting more contradictory emotions than Georgian romanticism. By the time the family left Sidcup in 1947, Adcock had developed preferences which anticipate her own mature verse with its mixture of the sinister and the psychologically extraordinary event, its often deceptively colloquial, conversational tone, its images of female entrapment and male control: she had a love for ballads like 'The Highwayman', was 'hooked on' 'The Lady of Shallott', the songs in William Morris's *The Hollow Land* and more sinister poems like Browning's 'Porphyria's Lover', 'with its deliciously murderous frisson' (B. 349).

Adcock herself came full circle in 1993 with 'The Pilgrim Fathers' which, after fifty years, ironically 'commemorates' her winning a Gold Star at school in 1943 for an epic poem about the Pilgrim Fathers. Adcock charges her nine-year-old self with neglect of issues concerning colonization, introducing her favourite devices of negation, and an external interlocutor or authority figure such as an inspector or school teacher:

> ...'Miss Adcock, perhaps you could explain
>
> your position as regards colonialism.
> Here you are, a New Zealander in Surrey,
> describing the importation of new values
> to America. Does this cause you any worry?'

(*Poems*, 258)

Mocking the old fashioned ballad form of her school poem – 'no one asked me to expatiate on / my reasons for employing a refrain' – she then questions the implied sexism of 'Pilgrim

17

Fathers': 'a patriarchal expression, you'll agree'. But mock-deflation yields to the child's simple pleasures: 'I liked the sound of it, is all I'd have said / if they'd questioned me. I did it for the rhyme' (*Poems*, 259). 'The Pilgrim Fathers' both sardonically critiques her childish achievement, ignorant then of the political correctness that movements such as feminism and postcolonialism now require, yet reinforces creative enjoyment, such as in working out the rhyme scheme. In these different ways the poem touches on Adcock's personal voyage of the intervening fifty years.

Adcock's rural idyll was only ever an interlude. When her father learned that he had obtained a university lectureship in Wellington the family left in early 1947 for New Zealand. The world in which she had felt at one, both within the family circle and in the semi-rural environments of Leicestershire and Surrey that she loved, was shattered. It was exchanged for a 'New World', her land of origin where, paradoxically, she felt increasingly a stranger.

NEW ZEALAND AND THE DIVIDED SELF: 1947–1963

The theory of the diasporic imaginary argues that when the individual is wrenched from the homeland, the creation of a fantasy 'imaginary homeland' occurs to compensate for the loss. Vijay Mishra states,

> ...the moment of 'rupture' is transformed into a trauma round an absence that because it cannot be fully symbolised becomes part of the fantasy itself.... Imaginary homelands are constructed from the space of distance to compensate for a loss occasioned by an unspeakable trauma.[9]

For Adcock, departure from Britain at the end of the war to return to New Zealand was such a moment, full of inconsolable loss:

> For months I walked through the sparkling, frozen, record-breaking winter of 1946–47 seeing and experiencing things for the last time: our garden; the den I'd constructed there, with its painstakingly woven lattice-work of twigs; the ducks; the black cat we'd adopted; the carol service and Christmas party at school; conspiracies with Barbara and farewell visits to other friends; the dazzling, level snow on the school playing fields, where I waded ankle-deep inscribing

my name in gigantic capitals; my elm tree, every twig encased in glittering, rattling ice. It was all over (RB, 12).

The problems of departure were intensified for thirteen-year-old Adcock who was at that transitional period when all of life is more agonizing and separations are painfully suffered. She continues: 'When did childhood and adolescence begin? Was it then, with the last and most devastating betrayal?' Eva Hoffman, who moved from war-torn Poland to America with her family at the same age, writes of a similar anguish due to loss in *Lost in Translation*.[10] For Adcock, the trauma endured for years; she dreamed about going back 'and in this dream I'd walk up this hill and see the village where we lived'; such euphoric images of return reinforced her attachment to England.[11] Paradoxically, in those unsettled years of living in a war zone, she had found happiness, whereas returning to the 'safe haven' of New Zealand was disorienting. Severance from a country which she soon mythologized as the imaginary homeland finally led her to review her life and change her direction.

Adcock experienced not just a loss of childhood innocence, but also displacement of her youthful expectations about belonging, already decisively formed in relation to her British location. She says: 'I learned to live with an almost permanent sense of free-floating, unfocused nostalgia, and with the combination of crushed humility and confident arrogance that comes from not quite belonging' (RB, 12). At the time, returning seemed like an exhilarating move forward into the destiny that awaited her: reunion with her New Zealand relatives, particularly her mother's family in Drury, attendance at secondary school, Wellington Girls' College, and then at Victoria University of Wellington where her gift for languages took her into a study of Classics for an MA. She briefly enjoyed a student existence interrupted by marriage at the age of eighteen and then motherhood. In the mid-1950s she began publishing poetry. Within five years her marriage to Alistair Campbell was over; she left Wellington for Dunedin in 1958, taking the younger of their two sons, Andrew, with her, and leaving the older, Gregory, with Alistair and his new wife Meg. Working first as a junior lecturer in the Department of Classics, and then as a librarian in the University of Otago library, she stayed there for five years. A succession of relationships culminated in a brief but traumatic second marriage to the New Zealand writer, Barry Crump, before she left for the UK.

These developments, in which Adcock's personal and 'professional' lives ran in uneasy tandem culminating in her decision to emigrate, receive minimal attention in her first volume, *The Eye of the Hurricane*. The only explicit references to her life are in three poems, 'Invocation for Gregory', 'For Andrew' and 'For a Five-Year-Old', the opening, mid-collection, and concluding poem respectively. Indeed this first collection is notable for its 'placelessness' and lack of topicality.[12] The dearth of specific reference to location suggests that it can be read as Adcock's private meditation on her sense of alienation and her refusal to negotiate a place for herself within her surroundings. Coding her conflicts through a series of depersonalizing strategies, the silences and omissions which constitute this gaping hole become as significant as the thirty-five poems on the page. The recurring themes of dislocation, separation and frustration also conjure up the psychological impasse which is at the heart of the collection's first three poems.

'Invocation for Gregory' explores a conflict between love for her son and a wish to detach herself from parenting, reminiscent of Sylvia Plath's ambivalence about marriage and motherhood, as in her early poems addressed to a sleeping baby, 'Winter Trees' or 'Morning Song'.[13] Adcock's commendation of her first-born to the care of the elements –

> Now that I, with voice nor hand,
> cannot touch him with my care,
> I deputise it to the wind:
>
> (*TEOH*, 7; A. 127)

– is underlaid by a frustration expressed through paradox and anomaly:[14] the wind offers 'passive cool affection'. Her searing comment, 'while I burn in silence here', recalls Plath's 'gender anger'.[15] 'The Lover', which follows, also relies on generalizations. The subject who 'Always...would inhabit an alien landscape, / someone else's setting' (*TEOH*, 8; A. 128), is marked linguistically as male. But as the love affair 'in late childhood' is with 'an elm', recalling Adcock's ascent of the elm in 'The High Tree', this is a male persona adopted as a disguise.[16] The elm and 'a small creek' are signifiers of English landscapes by contrast to the 'bush valley' of New Zealand which 'he' 'walked with 'surly devotion'; the reluctant 'act of will' with which 'he would learn local names, claim kinship' suggests Adcock's difficulties with resettlement. The conclusion registers impasse as the lover is 'set apart', resigned to 'the city's plan' which will 'absorb him calmly'. In 'Summer is Gone', the third poem, despair at the loss of a familiar, loved landscape underpins the lament in the refrain, 'Summer is gone to another country'. The bleak vision polarizes alienating 'here', a place where

> ...trees have no more use for their leaves,
> branches are numb, the sap sealed in,
> the sky constricting, the wind unanchored:
>
> (*TEOH*, 9; A. 129)

and longed-for 'there' where 'moors of clouds' are 'banked in a dream's experienced landscape'.

Adcock's influences at this time were the classical poets she had studied at university like Propertius, Horace and Catullus; indeed her 'Note on Propertius 1.5' remains one of her most anthologized pieces. She had already discovered the rhythms of Blake, Milton, Donne, Goethe and Eliot. Later, English poets who handle precise verse forms with grace and exactness became important influences when she was experimenting with the formal patterns of rhyme and metre. Models for Adcock's colloquial, wry, ironic voice can be found in Horace and Auden, while her treatment of danger in love, disappointment and exhilaration in male-female relationships owes much to Robert Graves. In a poem dedicated to Graves, 'Wooing the Muse' (*TEOH*, 35; A. 133), she illustrates his advocation that life's passions should find a counterpart in art, for 'the poet's art is that of the seducer'.

Yet these influences do not completely explain the sense of dislocation in her work, the destabilizing of fixed positions and the subliminal presence of warring forces. Other poems in this first volume show love and desire as blighted by hostile and threatening natural forces, suggestive of an underlying moral Puritanism. The eponymous poem, 'The Eye of the Hurricane', which introduces a fantasized, idyllic Mediterranean setting, beset by storm, uses the oxymoron 'sick desire' to parallel human destructiveness with the onslaught of nature: 'Soon, / As we look towards each other in sick desire . . . / the impatient wind will turn inwards and choke us.' (*TEOH*, 25; A. 131) In one of the finest, 'Incident', intimacy introduces a series of disorienting transitions. The speaker, sitting 'warm on the sand' with her lover, 'talking and smoking', falls asleep; the sudden shift into the unconscious is imaged surrealistically as disappearing underground to a primordial space;

> It was all the cave-myths, it was all
> the myths of tunnel or tower or well–
> Alice's rabbit hole into the ground,
> or the path of Orpheus: a spiral staircase
> to hell, furnished with danger and doubt.

(Poems, 19–20)

Dream turns into nightmare; on waking the horror intensifies as she observes him, 'waiting for the lapping tide to take me: / watching, and lighting a cigarette.'

Elsewhere in her exploration of family and sexual relationships Adcock turns to the European universalizing medium of fable and fairy tale as objective correlatives for her situation. Many are critiques of the gendered stereotypes of myth and legend, suggesting that her quarrel with gendered roles is as pronounced as her unhappiness with locale: 'The Beanstalk' celebrates the masculine heroic ability to transcend earthliness:

> Pythagorean Jack
> swung the stringy ladder
> from earth to sky and back.

(TEOH, 18; A. 129)

but undermines this superhuman effort by wryly observing: 'in the upper air / nothing dwells but weather'. Jack's collapse is observed from a bird's eye view:

> . . . on the fallen beanstalk
> the hen, with yellow eye,
> clucks a dull derision
> of ladders to the sky.

(A. 130)

Similarly, the gendered stereotypes of fairy tale are interrogated and playfully reinforced in the hyperbolic contrast between beauty and the beast in 'Beauty Abroad': 'Beauty goes / trembling through the gruesome wood'. This re-narrativization of the fable as a modern allegory of seduction emphasizes the effect on Beauty's tender heart of the beast's misery, not his strength as fearfully anticipated. 'He lays his muzzle on her hand, / says "Pity me!" and "Can you understand?"' The poem concludes that passive manipulation is as effective as brute force because 'The beast, like any hero, knows / sweet talk can lead him to *la belle chose*' (*Poems*, 17).[17] Adcock elsewhere reverses the passive heroine and forceful hero stereotypes by introducing mythological, all-powerful female figures. The heroine of 'The Witch' reduces her 'latest client' who takes the 'thick drops [which] from the alembic fall / into a flask' and then 'shivers and seems to shrink'; But the poem also demystifies arcane knowledge as innocuous domestic spells: 'Purely experimental, her drugs home-made' (*TEOH*, 20; A. 130).

Adcock's poems about her sons are among her best known and appreciated for their tender sentiments, yet their troubling implications have been largely overlooked. Emma Neale, however, in analyzing 'Invocation for Gregory' as a prayer to the elements, argues that the poem's conflicted attitude towards parenthood is representative of the wider tensions which Adcock will face:

> ...the struggle for self definition which must take place outside domestic exigencies. The poem prefigures journeys, restlessness and separation from family, already disruption to and redefinition of home.... This tension between rest and restlessness is an opposition inherent in the title (and eponymous poem) of [*The Eye of the Hurricane*]... any peace achieved is equivocal, reflecting a temporary state.[18]

This scepticism about her role and the theme of betrayal of child-mother trust is echoed in the domestic setting of 'For a Five-Year-Old', the collection's final poem.[19] The speaker explains to her son, Andrew, who has found a snail in his room 'that it would be unkind to leave it there /...we must take care / That no one squashes it'. In the second stanza she reflects on her own acts of destruction:

> I see, then, that a kind of faith prevails:
> your gentleness is moulded still by words
> from me, who have trapped mice and shot wild birds,
> from me, who drowned your kittens, who betrayed

your closest relatives, and who purveyed
the harshest kind of truth to many another.

(*Poems*, 21)

The concluding lines reinforce the ironic pose of this ambivalent
maternalism. 'But that is how things are: I am your mother,/ and
we are kind to snails' (*Poems*, 21). As important as the fact of
motherhood is the power of words to 'mould' and teach a 'faith'
to which she only partially subscribes. This self-reflexive
equivocation characterizes Adcock's relationship to language
as well as to her sons. But the tension between what is expected
of her and her ambivalence about this role, both in these two
poems and the central poem, 'For Andrew', are reflections on
rather than any resolution to its principal problematic. To give
new expression to this innate sense of division, Adcock turns to
the genres of fantasy and the surreal and the discontinuous
processes associated with them. Two poems illustrate this
departure: 'Unexpected Visit' and 'Regression'.

In writing on trauma and disorder, Freud, and following him
Lacan, speak of how language is often inadequate to convey the
event; and that the sense of structural dislocation is 'uncanny'.
The traumatized subject is exiled from the realm in which the
instincts hold sway, and abandoned within the world of
necessary invention, for trauma is a state of 'not being at home
with oneself'. The alteration in consciousness produces a
'conflict in the form of unrestrainable affect which breaks
through the frame of chronologically ordered time and
habituated space that has seemed to shelter and make safe the
human being, displacing these...'.[20] Trauma occurs when
events not assimilated at the time recur belatedly, possessing
the subject in ways which cause fright and an alteration or
dislocation of perspective.[21] The disorientation apparent in
Adcock's poems about disturbing events or states of mind,
showing reality as disjunctive and dissociated, suggests affi-
nities with some forms of writing associated with post-traumatic
stress disorder, such as that of post-Holocaust survivors, in
which the familiar becomes strange and conversely the strange
becomes familiar.

'Unexpected Visit' recounts the 'uncanny' structural disloca-
tion of the subject in relation to her surroundings. Adcock opens
with the trope of *occupatio* (negation) to represent an unwanted

state of affairs: the inexplicable habitation of an undesirable location is represented as slippage from the normal:[22]

> I have nothing to say about this garden.
> I do not want to be here, I can't explain
> what happened. I merely opened a usual door
> and found this.

(Poems, 20)

Line breaks working against the phrasal flow and medial pauses stressing breaks between phrases and sentences, reinforce stylistically this surrealist opening, suggestive of the dislocation caused by the response to trauma. The non-committal enigmatic 'arrival' – 'I do not want to be here/... But here I am' – suggests reluctant acceptance of the literal return of the traumatic event against the subject's will. Furthermore, after opening 'the usual door' the speaker discovers none of the familiar reference points exist. Not only are 'The gracious vistas, / the rose-gardens and terraces... all wrong', nature itself is askew. Alienation increases with the loss of temporal, visual perspectives: 'under a sky so dull I cannot read / the sundial' where 'there is no / horizon behind the trees, no sun as clock / or compass'. The response to this defamiliarized normality, recalls 'The Lover', for it involves isolation, passivity, reduced horizons. Unlike the lover, however, who meditates on the loss of 'challenging lust', the narrator's behaviour in 'Unexpected Visit' is consistent with the 'erasure' of her reality: she seeks an inconspicuous toolshed, 'somewhere among the formal hedges/ or hidden behind a trellis', as if desiring an embryonic, foetal position 'among the rakes and flowerpots/and sacks of bulbs'. Nothing occurs beyond the cognitive experience of waiting, for 'Whatever happens /may happen anywhere'; and the opportunity for survival by being 'at least/...warm and dry' completes this scenario of passive resignation.[23] The conscious, waking experience of disorientation in 'Unexpected Visit' can be contrasted to the nightmarish awakening in 'Incident' which reinforces intense fear at the loss of self, already expressed through dream and nightmare. This elision between waking and dreaming will characterize some of Adcock's best poems written after she had left New Zealand.

In 'Regression', the trope of reversal is the means of defamiliarization, providing direction to disorientation; this vision, verging on the comical, is an absurdist fantasy.

25

All the flowers have gone back into the ground.
              ... they suddenly wound
the film of their growth backwards. We saw them shrink
from blossom to bud to tiny shoot,
down from the stem and up from the root.
Back to the seed, brothers. It makes you think.

(Poems, 25)

The recording voice, representing collective 'we', mocks the human capacity to be disconcerted by this image of the world-gone-wrong, 'a conspiracy of inverted birth', which when taken to its logical conclusion, returns us to our pre-lapsarian condition, and asks: 'how shall we / endure as we deserve to be,/foolish and lost on the naked skin of the earth?' (Poems, 26). The tongue-in-cheek, moralizing, essentially sardonic pose in recording the disjunctive event, is the upbeat, celebratory counterpart to the numbed, passive speaker in 'Unexpected Visit', 'The Lover', and 'Incident'. The technique of using a collective voice anticipates subversive 'public' poems written in the 1980s like 'From the Demolition Zone', 'A Hymn to Friendship' and 'Smokers for Celibacy'. The perception of disorder in the structure of reality, which can be traced to her own experiences of trauma in poems like 'Unexpected Visit' and which inspire a surreal vision, foreshadows post-cultural poems like 'Last Song.'

Although some poems in The Eye of the Hurricane suggest that her apprenticeship to the muse is ongoing, the collection as a whole identifies Adcock as having 'arrived'. It introduces a range of different styles, voices, and genres, demonstrates an ability to blend classical allusion with colloquial vigour and, as New Zealand critics recognized, reveals her accomplishment in presenting with unusual assurance domestic situations as well as exploring more public themes. What the early readings of her work did not discern so clearly, because her poise and classical veneer functioned effectively as a protective screen, is the nature of the turbulence which she was trying to bring under control, the psychological divisions which were to emerge as a conflict between two locations and nations. This first volume discreetly, even insidiously, maps out the problematic psychological territory which Adcock only begins to occupy more fully after she has left New Zealand. From the mid-1960s she begins to address from an external position, those issues of nation, home and belonging which had already begun to obsess her.

26

3

Home, Identity and Belonging: England 1963–1974

Adcock's first decade in England, following her arrival in January 1963, saw her striking out in crucial new directions, and, by developing new allegiances and discovering other landscapes and countries, beginning to redraw the map of her identity.[1] Nevertheless the 'love affair' with England, a source of nostalgia and longing during sixteen years after the family's return to New Zealand in 1947, required radical reassessment. Had this been a running away as she later claimed?[2] Now she realized she was a New Zealander, not just 'someone who happened to have lived in New Zealand' (LOW, 103); conscious that accent signals nationality, she implies her ambivalence through clandestine adjustments in 'Immigrant':

> I clench cold fists in my Marks and Spencer's jacket
> and secretly test my accent once again:
> St James's Park; St James's Park; St James's Park.

> *(Poems, 111)*

The uneven process of relocation which exposed such assumptions about her identity and national belonging meant that initially her creative powers were drained: she says 'the whole process of adjustment to a different culture set my writing back dismally for a time' (B. 356).

The Eye of the Hurricane, published in New Zealand in 1964, was unavailable in England, but Adcock soon became known for her poetry, at first through meetings of the Group at Edward Lucie-Smith's house in London, where she met the Australian-born poet, Peter Porter, the BBC producer of poetry programmes, George MacBeth, and others like Martin Bell and Alan

Brownjohn; then gradually on the national scene. The Group offered an entrée to the larger literary milieu, providing the contacts needed for submitting her work to British magazines; it also offered her a critically responsive audience, for its workshop approach, based around the principles of close reading and a Leavisite engagement with the text, gave her the opportunity to read aloud and examine her work more closely in the light of members' comments.

Undoubtedly, though, as Julian Stannard has pointed out,[3] Adcock's cool, restrained style and use of classical principles were innately in tune with the Augustan ethos of post-Movement poetry with its liking for understatement, and deflation of rhetorical pretension. Her private, domestic orientation, her preoccupation with relationships and dreaming, sometimes bordering on the surreal, suited the post-war vogue for the modest and unpretentious, and the emphasis on the individual's experience which poets like Plath and Larkin had fashioned. Although Adcock arrived too late for inclusion in the Group anthology, she became respected as one of its few significant female voices.[4] But after the Group had dissolved and Martian poetry made waves in the late 1970s, and women's poetry took off in the 1980s, Adcock's work has been differentiated from this movement. Only upon publication of her *Selected Poems* in 1983 were issues of nation, identity and exile identified in her work, associated with a deeper restlessness and an openness to places.[5] The complete canon contained in *Poems 1960–2000* offers even stronger grounds for reading Adcock's work in relation to contemporary discourses of migration, diaspora and multicultural formation.

Despite her presence at the centre of mainstream poetry, as represented by the Group, Adcock was, at first, psychologically on the margins of British culture. Work from her first decade which manifests rootlessness, dislocation and other psychological effects of exile can be read in relation to other diasporic writers like V.S. Naipaul and 'traveller writers' like the New Zealander, Janet Frame, who visited England in the 1960s.[6] She has been identified with a tradition of New Zealand expatriate writers, some of whom returned to New Zealand: Katherine Mansfield, Robin Hyde, and in the 1960s, the poets Kevin Ireland, Hubert Witheford, Basil Dowling and W.S. Oliver.[7] Yet her decision to settle permanently in England, so exercising a choice about belonging, differentiates her from writers like Dan Davin, Katherine Mansfield or Robin Hyde, who in exile turned to their memories of their original homeland as a source of inspiration. For Adcock 'home' was already a contested term and to re-establish a sense of 'home' and belonging required at first a rejection of New Zealand as is manifested in key poems in *High Tide in the Garden*. Nor could she at first identify with England. The image which she had nurtured during her intervening years in New Zealand was a romanticized ideal trapped in childhood fantasy and, unsurprisingly, failed to find full expression in her writing upon her return.

Adcock's predicament conforms to the double-edged paradigm of diaspora theory, as outlined by Avtah Brah, that diaspora creates the desire to rediscover and rewrite home in order to understand separation from it through exile or migration.[8] Her double dislocation and split-consciousness meant that poetry about either nation – New Zealand or England – would initially be mediated through a search for new modes of identity. These came from discovering new places by travelling, recalling childhood memories of both countries and finding her Anglo-Saxon and Irish ancestors. Nevertheless, the psychological need to give voice to her rejection of New Zealand, then to write the country back into the narrative of her life, remained. The tension between the two different sources of identity – that of home and nation (where she was born and where family ties are strongest) and that of her 'homing desire' and belonging (to her place of ancestry, and of her destiny) – would dominate: 'the question of my national identity has influenced, infected and to some extent even distorted the course of my adult life'.[9] Departure from New Zealand, then, initiated a reworking and rewriting of her life story.

Three volumes helped establish Adcock as a mainstream poet in Britain: *Tigers* (1967), *High Tide in the Garden* (1971) and *The Scenic Route* (1974). Collectively they show a substantial expansion of her mood, subject matter and range. Adcock articulates her negative responses to New Zealand in the context of newly acquired reference points and widened horizons offered by proximity to Europe and the encounter with different cultures. Travel poetry develops her outsider eye as tourist, as the title *The*

Scenic Route suggests, as well as fostering an attitude of detachment that critics have, at times, found wanting. Yet when travel is linked with a personal quest, such as her search for the graves of her Ulster ancestors in 'Please Identify Yourself', the engagement points to new directions. All three volumes reveal the culture shock that comes with exile: of readjusting childhood memories to the newly discovered reality of England, of discovering the 'irreconcilable' or 'irresolvable' division between two worlds as the problematic, 'prior' claims of her New Zealand connections emerge. Adcock says 'I did choose to leave New Zealand when I was at last free to make a choice, and England has been my home ever since. But by then there was another "but." '[10] Returning to a place of childhood happiness led to the discovery that crucial aspects of her identity, a complex nexus of origins, kinship ties and culture, had already been formed; her family and her past meant that New Zealand continued to exert a subliminal pull, despite her initial euphoria at having 'escaped'.

TIGERS (1967)

If the poems of *The Eye of the Hurricane*, in their tactical use of silence (about the local landscape) and indirection (coding her dissatisfaction through masculine personae and the stereotypes of legend and fairy tale), suggest Adcock's psychological dislocation when living in New Zealand, then those of her second volume, *Tigers*, published in 1967, convey little more than the 'enigma of arrival'. *Tigers* contains thirteen new poems, alongside thirteen of the most admired poems of *The Eye of the Hurricane*. Classic anthology pieces, 'Note on Propertius 1.5', 'For a Five-Year-Old', 'Incident', introduced her to a new reading public as a poet with an accessible, conversational style, interested in children, relationships, and dreaming. Adcock signals continuity by placing 'For a Five-Year-Old', the final poem of the earlier volume, as the opening poem of her new book. 'For Andrew' is once more located centrally, the thirteenth of twenty-six poems, so suggesting her son's centrality in her life.[11] But given her expatriate status in England, the overlapping of the two volumes, of new with old

30

poems, suggests tentativeness, an as yet unexplored idea of 'homecoming'. Arrival and departure, it would seem, are not yet fully separated states.

The disassociation and eventlessness of 'Unexpected Visit' is counterpointed by the 'eventfulness' of *Tigers'* second poem, 'Miss Hamilton in London'. Notable because places and people are named for the first time, the poem invites an autobiographical reading.[12] The solitary Miss Hamilton:

> ...visited several bookshops, spent an hour
> in the Victoria and Albert Museum (Indian section),
> and walked carefully through the streets of Kensington
>
> (*Poems*, 22).

Other nations are named: 'Arriving home, she wrote a letter to someone/in Canada, as it might be, or in New Zealand'. This topographical realism and minutely recorded account of the spinster's day is stylistically mediated through flat, measured phrasing and Adcock's favourite rhetorical devices of *litotes* (understatement) and *occupatio* (negation). The opening line contains a double negation: 'It would not be true to say she was doing nothing'; the second stanza opens, 'Nor did she lack human contacts'; the third, 'A full day, and not unrewarding.' The synchronization of line and syntactic unit is also notable. This syntactic tautness is released in the single extended sentence of the third and final stanza which effects a climactic transition from the everyday and familiar into mysterious, unknowable night-time. She

> then went to bed; where, for the hours of darkness,
> she lay pierced by thirty black spears
> and felt her limbs numb, her eyes burning,
> and dark rust carried along her blood.
>
> (*Poems*, 22)

To interpret the image of the spinster being pierced using the stereotype of gender (sexual penetration), imagery of the Passion (equivalent to a crucifixion) or ethnic stereotyping ('black spears' and 'rust in the blood' suggesting a contaminating encounter with the Other leading to a loss of ethnic purity), is to over-determine these lines. Like 'Unexpected Visit', the passivity of the subject and the unreleased tension of 'her limbs numb', 'her eyes burning' and 'dark rust', are waking experiences, authorized and reinforced by the realistic detail elsewhere in the poem. Paradoxically the hours of darkness create a conscious state, but with the heightened mesmeric sense of passivity and immobility that is associated with sleep: whether this experience is empowering or not is unanswered. The inconsequential detail of the spinster's daytime activities switches to the enormous consequence of night-time, as her seemingly automated behaviour is transformed into sensations that appear overwhelming. Is this a representation of Adcock's entry into a new world, as yet incompletely inhabited? The power of the poem lies partly in its repression of information, its refusal to yield any clue.

The meaning of 'Miss Hamilton in London' becomes clearer when it is read with reference to 'The Lover' and to their strategic location as the second poem in each volume: 'The Lover' follows 'Invocation for Gregory' in *The Eye of the Hurricane*;[13] 'Miss Hamilton' follows 'For a Five-Year-Old'. In each case the shift from addressing a child to the adult's subjectivity invokes the generational gap between Adcock and her sons. Both are about the adult's loss of intimacy; read in sequence they create a narrative. The lover can only 'claim kinship / By an act of will'; although he searches for the lost love, he cannot find it: 'the climax never came' and 'the challenging lust ebbed back unfulfilled'. (*TEOH*, 8; A.128) Miss Hamilton, who has never known love, has no need for such an act of will; she is in the 'correct' landscape, the one that the lover desires and from which, like the narrator of 'Unexpected Visit', he is alienated, where places and names – signifiers and signifieds – are in harmony. Her waking immolation, a brutal intimacy, is arguably the climax that the lover desired but did not achieve. That being pierced by thirty spears may equally be a climax of rapture as of torture suggests the re-enactment of trauma (in a different location) where pain is interchangeable with pleasure, of release through primitive sensation from the psychological stasis of her mundane, everyday life.

'Note on Propertius 1.5', one of the finest poems in *The Eye of the Hurricane*, which in *Tigers* follows 'Miss Hamilton', recreates a bedroom scene from Roman love poetry in which 'possession / is a rare theme' (*Poems*, 14). This counterpoints the piercing and burning of Miss Hamilton. The poem's question, if Propertius was 'tear-sodden and jealous' does this mean that Cynthia was 'inexorably callous?', asks for appreciation of Cynthia's subjectivity. Cynthia's singular self-fulfilment in art recalls Miss Hamilton's self-sufficiency: 'she, so gay a lutanist, was known / to stitch and doze a night away, alone'. Furthermore the ambivalence that passion arouses in Cynthia, matches that of Miss Hamilton's 'intimate' experience: Propertius 'gently roused her sleeping mouth to curses'. The poem concludes with another image of the yielding female – 'and she compliant to his every wish' – because, as 'the conventions reassert their power:/ The apples fall and bruise, the roses wither', this is yet another image of transience.

Other poems in *Tigers* continue the theme of nocturnal disorder introduced in 'Miss Hamilton in London' from more comic, playful angles. Night-time and dreaming, what Herrick once called 'the civil wilderness of sleep', are potent zones for such disturbed feelings, imaged as the unexpected event, and Adcock's poems of dreaming and nightmare are emblematic of psychological dislocation in general.[14] Disorientation leading to confusion between waking and sleeping constitutes the surreal atmosphere of 'Hauntings', a bizarre poem about 'transformations', with intrusive nocturnal figures who traipse through a friend's house. Characteristically, Adcock's waking comments interpenetrate the dream content: 'Where are we this time? On what planet?'. The absurdity of the comic climax lies in the confusion between the two states:

> At last I think I have woken up.
> I lift my head from the pillow, rejoicing.
> The alarm-clock is playing Schubert:
> I am still asleep. This is too much.

> (*Poems*, 28)

Another dream poem, 'I Ride on My High Bicycle', contains deft transitions between contrasting settings and physical sensations: the dreamer rides on her bike 'into a sooty Victorian city / of colonnaded bank buildings, / horse troughs, and green marble fountains'; 'unexpected sunshine' appears and, 'There below lies Caroline Bay, / its red roofs and its dazzling water.' The violent intrusion of reality, imaged as brutal entrapment, is classic Adcock incongruity:

but something has caught me; around my shoulders
I feel barbed wire; I am entangled.

It pulls my hair, dragging me downwards;...
I struggle weakly; and wake, of course.

(Poems, 26)

'The Water Below' with its multiple points of view began as a dream. Recorded as a waking experience it conflates the house and consciousness as places of occupation. Unlike the spiralling disorientation created by the perverse landscape in 'Unexpected Visit', here the perceived disturbance to normality is accepted with apparent equanimity:

This house is floored with water,
wall to wall, a deep green pit,
still and gleaming, edged with stone. ...
It will have to be rebuilt:...

(Poems, 30)

Yet there is anxiety about the water's pervasiveness: 'But I am sure the water / would return; would never go.' The collective voice and parenthetical allusion to the Lord's Prayer which follow, suggest the water below is analogous to the dangerous, unknown, even evil territory of the unconscious. The poem concludes that this is an unchanging, primordial state:

Always beneath the safe house
lies the pool, the hidden sea
created before we were.

Between these opening observations and concluding assertions is a confessional reminiscence:

Under my grandmother's house
in Drury, when I was three,
I always believed there was
water; lift up the floorboards
and you would see it—a lake,
a subterranean sea.

This autobiographical voice precipitates the transition to the collective view that deep water which 'is not easy to drain', aligned with unconscious powers and primordial danger, requires Christian prayer as protection. The poem demands an allegorical reading: the split between the conscious belief 'above'

34

the floorboards that there is a pool of water below them, and the empirical knowledge that there is no water below, suggests the divisions between reality and imagination or the conscious and unconscious realms. The child's misapprehension nevertheless implies that the presence of the unconscious (i.e. water) is essential for existence, despite claims that it is also dangerous. Her assertion of the primacy of the hidden world with its threatening connotations argues that belief, however idiosyncratic, can overturn evidence of one's sight.

> True, I played under the house
> and saw only hard-packed earth, ...
> That was different: below
> I saw no water. Above,
> I knew it must still be there,
> waiting.

The narrator's defiance of the logic of the senses both celebrates the imagination's powers and anticipates Adcock's desire for self-relocation. The poem's central premise: 'This house is floored with water. . . / It will have to be rebuilt', perhaps an analogue to her psyche acknowledged as in need of reconstruction, might point to the predisposition to disorientation found in dream poems such as 'Hauntings' and 'I Ride on my High Bicycle'.

'The Water Below' contains Adcock's first references to her early home and family – her grandmother's house in Drury – anticipating other poems about her childhood like 'Script', 'Going Back' and 'Kuaotunu'. It exposes the dichotomies experienced by her three-year-old self. Significantly the idea of 'home' as being paradoxically fraught with danger – what Freud calls *unheimlich* or *ungemutlich* – is the lesson of the all-encompassing hidden water, analogous to the dark power emanating from the unconscious realm. It also anticipates the self-assessment made upon her first return to New Zealand in the eponymous poem of *The Inner Harbour*.

'The Water Below', like 'Being Blind' (*Poems*, 41), another poem which explores the challenge to cognitive powers, here when the speaker imagines herself blind, and others in *The Eye of the Hurricane* which privilege the concealed world of the imagination and the pernicious presence of the unconscious, lie outside the poetic tradition in New Zealand which, from the

1930s to the end of the 1960s, was mainly concerned with defining responses to the New Zealand referent. On a more political level one could argue that Adcock's is a minority discourse which contests those hegemonic ones which lead to 'claims for cultural supremacy and historical priority'.[15] The very lack of a nationalistic discourse in Adcock's work suggests a questioning of a central precept of colonization, hard won in Anglophone New Zealand, that colonial habitation should be 'homely'. Certainly the collective voice's fear for the child's misunderstanding of the relationship between appearances and 'reality' in 'The Water Below', argues that the desire to rewrite her origins and the narrative of her life required a deliberate intervention in the past and its epistemological traditions. The divisions it explores can be read in terms of Homi Bhabha's theory of culture, that the 'originary' is always open to translation through language, a 'process of alienation and of secondariness *in relation to itself*', that 'it can never be said to have a totalized prior moment of being or meaning – an essence'.[16] Adcock's restaging of the past from a minority perspective, by introducing other 'incommensurable cultural temporalities', interrogates tradition in that it inhibits immediate 'access to an originary identity or a "received" tradition'.[17]

This seminal poem, like 'Miss Hamilton', opens the floodgates to writing which brims over with names of places and people, of sights seen, of the observed detail of locations and the external world of nature, civilization and history. As significant meditations on the powers that both define yet complicate Adcock's purchase on reality, this 'reconstruction' of the place of the imagination in terms of oppositions (below and above; asleep and awake), releases her voice in the process of severing what she experienced as the cumbrous umbilical cord of her original homeland.

HIGH TIDE IN THE GARDEN (1971)

In Adcock's third volume, a significant reorientation of her perspective can be traced in five strategically located poems. Two named for New Zealand locations, 'Ngauranga Gorge Hill' and 'Stewart Island', concern her rejection of her country. Both are highly mediated: 'Ngauranga Gorge Hill' through the distancing mechanism of time, looking back on her younger self, and 'Stewart Island' through the contrasting perspective of those who choose to stay behind. They can be juxtaposed with two poems celebrating her East Finchley residence: 'Saturday' and 'The Trees'. These two pairs, with their contrasting New Zealand rural and English bourgeois landscapes, are separated by a fifth poem, 'On a Son Returned to New Zealand' (*Poems*, 44–45), a centrepiece creating the effect of a triptych; it links the other poems thematically and emotionally with its pathos and tenderness. Written in 1966, on the occasion of her son Gregory's return to his father in Pukera Bay (he had visited England with Adcock's mother and then Greece with Adcock), this poem introduces the theme of conflicting loyalties. The moment of parting leads to separate journeys, she to England, Gregory to New Zealand. Its handling of travel abroad as a form of self-relocation, including reconnecting to New Zealand, will be a significant feature of subsequent writing.

In 'Ngauranga Gorge Hill' Adcock's disaffection with New Zealand appears in the critical observations of her surroundings: Ngauranga Gorge outside Wellington consists of 'Nothing... but rock and gorse, gravel-/pits, and foxgloves' (*Poems*, 43); the velocity of the downward journey on her bike and the need to look ahead rationalize her dislike of the 'awkward landscape' and anticipate her flight as an adult:

> Heart in my pedals, down I would roar
>
> towards the sea; I'd go straight into it
> if I didn't brake. No time then to stare
> self-consciously at New Zealand vegetation,
> at the awkward landscape.

> (*Poems*, 43)

The poem introduces double-sided images of procreation: 'The bee in the foxglove, the mouth on the nipple,/ the hand between the thighs' (innocent 'nipples' and 'thighs' but stinging 'bees' and poisonous 'foxgloves'). Breeding is paradoxically associated with barrenness; her passivity is sourced to Wellington: 'For ten years/that city possessed me. In time it bred / two sons for me'. Disappointment is made explicit in the dismissive conclusion: 'I think it was a barren place'. In 'Stewart Island' the narrator apparently acquiesces with the hotel manager's wife's invitation:

'Look at all this beauty':

>   ...   True: there was a fine bay,
>   all hills and atmosphere; white
>   sand, and bush down to the sea's edge;

(Poems, 44)

This approval of the landscape is undermined; the wife ran off with a Maori fisherman and the mood darkens with the image of a seagull savagely tearing the narrator's son's head with its claws and beak and her terse rejection: 'I had already / decided to leave the country'.

'On a Son Returned to New Zealand' involves more complex positioning as Adcock redraws the binary map of migration with a new, triangulated geography: Athens, with its associations with the classical empire of Greece, is where mother and son part; Wellington and London their respective destinations. The comment, 'No one can be in two places at once' (*Poems*, 44), is imaged in the layout with indented first lines of each subsequent stanza suggesting their different trajectories. The return to New Zealand of her first born – 'my first invention' – stands in for the journey and homecoming she does not make and so links her presence in London to the land where family intimacy is implied by 'his father's house'. In defining Gregory as her emissary to a country which she no longer wishes to claim as her own, and a family in whose lives she remains involved, she repositions her earlier disaffection through the conflict of loyalties:

>   He was
>   already in his father's house, on the
>   cliff-top, where the winter storms roll across
>   from Kapiti Island, and the flax bends
>   before the wind. He could go no further.

(Poems, 45)

The finely judged penultimate line, 'He could go no further', dramatizes distance, separation and journey's end. Distance is further transformed into memory and son into symbol in the conclusion: 'He is my bright sea-bird on a rocky beach'.

The theme of successful habitation dominates the less problematically engaged London poems. In 'Saturday', the 'relocated' Fleur Adcock speaks from her East Finchley house:

> I am sitting on the step
> drinking coffee and
> smoking, listening to jazz.

(Poems, 45)

Her exultant mood overflows into affection for the external world:

> I am painting the front door
> with such thick juicy
> paint I could almost eat it.

The poem's typography with stanza breaks marked by stars suggests pauses, even the discontinuities of the absurd. Adcock's zany, fanciful humour, a happier outcome of the distortions caused by dreams, nightmares or hallucinations, now celebrates self-transformation. The final stanza reads:

> I am floating in the sky.
> Below me the house
> crouches among its trees like
> a cat in long grass.
> I want to stroke its roof-ridge
> but I think I can
> already hear it purring.

(Poems, 46)

Disembodied, she soars Chagall-like above the house, but the analogies between the house and the taut feline energy of the cat's crouch, between the roof ridge that she wishes to stroke and the cat's purr, suggest domestic intimacy and connectedness.

Similar images of burgeoning, transformative energy are at the heart of the single stanza comprising 'Trees' which opens with one of her favourite devices, a list, here also a litany of the English trees in her neighbourhood garden:

> Elm, laburnum, hawthorn, oak:
> all the incredible leaves expand
> on their dusty branches, like
> Japanese paper flowers in water,

(Poems, 47)

The poem's fluid movement mimics the profuseness of verdant growth that, as a canopy or shelter, seems to offer privacy and a haven.

These five poems which express Adcock's responses to relocation and her revision of ideas of home and belonging – dismissing one landscape while finding a new domestic space in another, linking the hemispheres through her son's journey back to New Zealand – define a process of assimilation to England with new possibilities of self-agency. They can be contrasted with 'A Surprise in the Peninsula', a fantasy or dream-like poem which can be read as a coda. Like the poems in *The Eye of the Hurricane*, 'A Surprise in the Peninsula' is placeless;[18] but the importance of place, as represented by a map, is the poem's most significant point. The narrator finds the pelt of a dead dog nailed onto her wall. On it

> was branded the outline of the
> peninsula, singed in thick black
> strokes into the fur: a coarse map.

(*Poems*, 38)

A town's position is 'marked by a bullet-hole' that goes through the wall. As with 'The Water Below' her attitude to this menacing sight is unemotional, measured. The 'surprise' for the reader becomes just this puzzling response: as C.K. Stead has written, 'A balance is maintained on a fine line between terror and the absurd; hysteria is just out of the picture, giving it its sharpness and point'.[19] This cool detachment allows her to cross this line and to ask whether the pelt is intended 'not as a warning, but a gift?' The poem's conclusion, 'And, scarcely shuddering, I drew / the nails out and took it with me', once more demonstrates Adcock's preoccupation with maps as a form of self-location. This is a leitmotiv in her work: the need to complete the map of her early childhood locale inspires 'Going Back'; her distress on hearing of her father's death in 'My Father' is projected through an inability to locate his home on the map of Manchester. The potential guidance which the map from nowhere offers in 'A Surprise in the Peninsula' overturns its grotesque appearance and sinister implications. The poem suggests that Adcock has armed herself for the journey to come.

THE SCENIC ROUTE (1974)

Adcock's fourth collection, *The Scenic Route*, resoundingly concludes her first decade of living diasporically: it exhibits expanded horizons and an asssured relocation. The title's implication of the traveller 'viewing' other landscapes and cultures anticipates the strengths and weaknesses of her mature work. Adcock by now is discovering and falling in love with places as she admits: 'I write a good deal about places; I have passionate relationships with them'.[20] When new or imaginary places stimulate a deeper problem or train of thought, or surprise or challenge her, they lead to fine poetry such as 'A Surprise in the Peninsula' or to the responses to Wordsworth's landscapes in *Below Loughrigg*. But some encounters are eventless, merely an occasion for writing a poem. Adcock's persona as a cool, aloof observer in such poems has led to criticisms of detached indifference, although an early adverse comment that she 'defines a world of attitudes...more often than feeling or emotions' was countered by New Zealand critics.[21] The traveller's curiosity and the lifestyle of a poet who travels frequently show her in less developed poems like 'Our Trip to the Federation' or 'In the Terai' (*Poems* 85, 108-09) as uninvolved, an ironic commentator or voyeuristic bystander; while her inclination to discover versions of herself through revisiting places, creates 'occasional' poems which record impressions like disengaged snapshots; for example, poems about her early schools in *The Incident Book* such as 'Scalford Again', 'Neston'.[22] Reviews of *Looking Back* point to this unevenness: one praises her ability for 'managing drama and incident' in the first section, but observes that the humour of the second is 'quirky and slight'.[23] Carol Rumens comments on 'a touch of archness' yet adds that Adcock will 'sooner or later' deliver a poem 'icily witty, or sheened with its own sinister erotic'.[24]

Most poems in *The Scenic Route* demonstrate how the pressures that accompanied Adcock's arrival still energize her work: her discovery of new territories, her encounter with her ancestral past and her readjustment to memories of her English childhood. Opening with two poems set in Northern Ireland and concluding with three titled with Northern Irish place-names – 'Near Creeslough', 'Kilmacrenan', 'Glenshane' – the volume shows resolution and 'arrival'. Within this frame of journeys in Northern Ireland are poems about other journeys, both genealogical and personal: the sea voyage of her grand-parents, Richey and Martha Brooks, who migrated from North-ern Ireland to New Zealand, her own trip in the early 1970s to visit a friend, Meg Sheffield, in Kathmandu, Nepal, and shorter trips like 'Kilpeck', written on the occasion of a poetry reading in Herefordshire.

A complex handling of geography emerges in the poetry of this first decade in England, particularly in this volume. By contrast to expatriate, modernist writers such as Katherine Mansfield and James Joyce, whose imaginations were liberated by a retrospective fixation on the abandoned homeland, Adcock's inspiration comes from discovery of new places and family connections in the British Isles; later these will reconnect her to New Zealand and its landscapes. Travel, and seeking out her maternal ancestors in *The Scenic Route*, enable her to overcome the migrant's fractured consciousness by discovering ethnic grounds of self-identification and exploring her con-flicted feelings about her past. As Stuart Hall says, 'identities are never completed, never finished; they are always, as subjectivity itself is, in process'.[25] The broadening of her referential frame-work from rejection of New Zealand, and detachment from the psychological conflict enable her to recognize and mediate in her verse other types of division. The 'subtle insights' into the Northern Irish situation in 'The Bullaun' and 'Please Identify Yourself' are due to her 'ambivalent sense of loyalty to England, New Zealand and Catholic and Protestant Ireland'.[26] Positioned outside the local frame, Adcock balances contradictory political and religious positions, aware of the impotency generated by civil strife. The all-important discovery of her Scots-Irish origins, her mother's forebears, in 'Please Identify Yourself', occurs in a region of conflict in which she recognizes that symbols of belief like the Bullaun, 'already theirs; a monument/ a functionless, archaic, pitted stone' (*Poems*, 60), make no difference.

Adcock's indebtedness appears in the dedication, 'For my Mother and in memory of her Mother and those others', and in two other poems about her mother's ancestors, 'Richey' and 'The Voyage Out', who journeyed from Northern Ireland to

New Zealand in the nineteenth century. An earlier gothic-grotesque poem, 'Grandma', about a nightmare concerning her newly deceased maternal grandmother, suggests a psychic dimension in this engagement with her mother's family. Its moral, 'even the dead want to be loved for their own sake' (*Poems*, 42), informs 'Over the Edge', an extraordinary poem of a single sentence which came to her in a dream.[27] Its claim of possession – 'All my dead people/seeping through the riverbank' – images the riverbank as a burial ground; while the 'pale brown' river water expresses her intimacy and empathy with the dead who are 'why I swim in the river' (*Poems*, 76). In representing a liminal state – the title hints at crossing from this world to the next – 'Over the Edge' anticipates Adcock's later obsessive search for her father's ancestors, also crucial to her acceptance of a doubled identity and nationality. As Stuart Hall says:

> But...ethnicity is a very specific and peculiar form of ethnic identity. It is located in a place in a specific history. It could not speak except out of a place, out of those histories. It is located in relation to a whole set of notions about territory, about where is home and where is overseas, what is close to us and what is far away.[28]

Just as moving to the UK made Adcock aware for the first time that she was in fact a New Zealander, and just as visiting Northern Ireland introduced her to her Scots-Irish, Protestant heritage, so arriving at more exotic destinations locates her in the broader categories of European, western and white. None of these locations suggest a homecoming. In poems written from Nepal the cultural and geographical distance of the Orient is suggested by the semantic density of the word 'foreign'. In 'Bodnath', 'I twirl the prayer-wheels, my foreign fingers / polishing their bronze by a fraction more'; conversely in 'External Service', the 'familiar' sound of a BBC broadcast she hears in Nepal is 'the foreign news' (*Poems*, 79–80). Foreignness also defines parts of Northern Ireland: 'Near Creeslough' opens 'I am in a foreign country' because 'Notices tell us in two old languages / (one mine) that this is Caisleán na dTúath, / Doe Castle' (*Poems*, 81). The emphasis on the semi-alien locale of Northern Ireland, where one of the languages is English, the

43

other Gaelic, raises the question of whether England is as yet 'home'. As a foreigner Adcock is a transient; visiting an alien country permits departure and cutting off rather than staying to adapt and understand. These traveller's observations can be contrasted to the powerfully imagined alienation of 'Foreigner', another 'nocturnally delivered' poem which blends conscious and unconscious voices. 'These winds bully me' was a phrase Adcock overheard while awake, but the lines – 'I am to lie down in a ditch / quiet under the thrashing nettles and pull the mud up to my chin.' – represent the 'slide back into the dream' (TWIH, 149). This restless movement, suggesting victimization, ceases with the abject subject's metamorphosis into a self-protective larva wrapped in mud, then imaged as a floating face and located, metaphorically, at the bottom of the nation:

> I shall lie sound-proofed in the mud,
> a huge caddis fly larva,
> a face floating upon Egyptian unguents
> in a runnel at the bottom of England.

(*Poems*, 107)

This enigmatic poem can be read as a fantasized image about the effects of exclusion, a comment on discrimination; its images of extreme subordination and self-protection speak for themselves.

Other poems in *The Scenic Route* chart a readjustment to the earlier notion of England as homeland: memories of her English childhood are tested out and the elements of fantasy reconciled to contemporary reality. Such 'correction' of childish memory through rediscovering familiar locations belongs to the jubilant expansion of psychological and emotional horizons under-pinning 'Saturday'. In 'St John's School' the forgotten church looming behind the school and the fearful power of the deity give her a shock:

> the church, that had hardly existed in my past,
>   ...   the church had grown:
> high on its huge mound it soared, vast;
> and God glared out from behind a tombstone.

(*Poems*, 70)

In the following decade she completed this process. The 'Schools' section in *The Incident Book* (1986) resulted from mentally revisiting some of the eleven schools in Kent, Surrey,

44

Leicestershire and Wiltshire that she had attended during the war: titles like 'Halfway Street Sidcup', 'St Gertrude's, Sidcup', 'Scalford School', 'Salfords, Surrey', 'Outwood', 'Earlswood', 'Scalford Again', 'Neston', 'Chippenham', 'Tunbridge Wells', recall names and details of masters and children, their comments and exchanges, lessons and activities. Such topographical realism, combined with a list, is characteristic of Adcock's scientific passion for precision. In recording moments of her childhood of 45 years ago, the litany of schools with their memories of voices and impressions anticipates her more recent autobiographical and genealogical reconstructions.

In Adcock's reconfiguring of 'home' in relation to 'abroad', through becoming accountable to more than one location, tradition and concept of home, relations between the sexes are also revalued. The success of 'Kilpeck' lies in the formal notation of features of setting and landscape to project the contrasting voices and positions of the woman and her male companion, as well as the minute adjustments required to sustain the precarious balance between them. Correlated with the action and accidents of travel, the exhilaration a new love affair is represented in the final two poems; in 'Kilmacrenan', when caught in a shower with her companion, the hailstorm which was earlier 'in my head' is externalized as 'real hail', drenching and transforming them into beings with a combined powerful intensity:

> we became patchworks of cold and hot,
> glowing, streaming with water,
> dissolving whatever dared to touch us.
>
> (*Poems*, 82)

In the glorious journey of 'Glenshane' the narrator's comment that 'Abandoning all my principles / I travel by car with you for days', is vicariously linked to her act of throwing salted peanuts into his mouth as he drives, 'at eighty miles an hour' (*Poems*, 82).

In keeping with the more retrospective character of this volume, separation from loved ones, friends and her younger, New Zealand self is strongly marked; in 'Moa Point' (*Poems*, 64) the youthful Adcock's determined rejection of a sea-slug handed to her by two male biologists, might anticipate that rejection of country and nation to come. Yet Adcock's expanding horizons, including the return to childhood memories and influences, soften this rejection. Recollection of harmonious family relationships in New Zealand extending over several generations leads to reflection on how her parents' skills have formed her own art. 'Script' recalls a family story about the freak transmission of sounds over the air waves that Adcock's great-grandmother and grandmother heard in Drury, 'Eighty years ago,/long before the wireless was invented' (*Poems*, 66); it develops into a reflection on her parents' talents, the genetic source of her own poetic gifts: her father tinkering, constructing loudspeakers, 'So my father's people were technicians, is that it? / And my mother's were communicators, yes?' That the past can interrupt and question the present is an unstated sub-text in this poem which concludes as a manifesto of her craft; the agricultural image of assimilation and dispersal is an apt metaphor for the way the creative process supersedes the tyranny of time:

> There will always
> be time to reassemble the frail components
> of this afternoon, to winnow the scattered sounds
> dropped into my range, and rescue from them
> a seed-hoard for transmission. There will be
> always the taking-in and the sending-out.

(Poems, 67)

Reminiscent of 'The Water Below' in its meditation on identity-formation through childhood and family, 'Script' suggests the different perspectives of memory, reflection and affectionate recreation involved in Adcock's gradually consolidating relationship with problematic New Zealand. Memory and enquiry into the lives of her colonial, pioneering forebears provide an autobiographical structure for interpreting her life story. Such anchorings of family history inform *The Scenic Route* which shows her tolerating ambiguity, juggling responses, and constructing new configurations of cultural syncreticism. Adcock's development of plural associations and subjectivities through increased travel and multiple destinations are now constitutive of major change.

4

To and Fro: Living in Diaspora

NEW DEPARTURES

Although the heightened activity in *The Scenic Route* confirms Adcock's ongoing acculturation to the northern hemisphere, her *annus mirabilis* came in 1979 with the publication of *The Inner Harbour* and *Below Loughrigg*. These mark significant developments: her first visit to New Zealand in 1975-6 after thirteen years; residencies in the Lake District (September 1977 to June 1978) as Arts Council Creative Writing Fellow at the Charlotte Mason College of Education in Ambleside, and in Newcastle (September 1979 to June 1981) as Northern Arts Literary Fellow at the universities of Newcastle and Durham.

Adcock's first journey 'home' established a 'to and fro' mode of existence of returning to New Zealand at least every two years. This return brought problems of 'belonging'; she was treated as a celebrity, having aroused public curiosity about her life and work. Elements of the earlier claustrophobia resurfaced when she was 'scorned as a Pom' and accused of lacking allegiance to the country of her birth.[1] New Zealand literary circles also reacted strongly to her exclusionary definition of nationality in her edition of *The Oxford Book of Contemporary New Zealand Poetry* (1982); she argued that writers (including herself) who chose to live abroad could not be called 'New Zealand poets'.[2] The residencies also had long-term repercussions: in 1979 Adcock resigned from her position in the Foreign and Commonwealth Office Library to become a full-time, free-lance writer. From now on she would live by judging poetry competitions, giving readings and talks, teaching on Arvon courses, writing, editing, and translating. She returned to her earlier interests in classical poetry, in 1983 publishing translations of medieval Latin lyrics, *The Virgin and the Nightingale* and in 1994, *Hugh Primas and the Archpoet*, an edition and translation of two twelfth-century 'Goliardic' poets, Hugh Primas of Orleans and the so-called Archpoet.

Adcock's growing reputation internationally as a poet also opened up new overseas connections: she visited Romania on writers' exchange trips sponsored by the British Council in 1984, 1987 and 1990 and taught herself the language; friendships with several Romanian poets whose work was censored by the Ceausescu regime resulted in *Orient Express*, her translation of poems by Grete Tartler (1989) and *Letters from Darkness*, translations of poems by Daniela Crasnaru (1991) (TWIH, 162–64).

RETURN, HOME AND NATION

The broadening of Adcock's horizons through the residencies in Newcastle and the Lake District, travel to Romania, visits to New Zealand and free-lance work, is marked by her increasing ability to traverse those boundaries which demarcate migration, diaspora and nation. Her poetry of the 1970s and 1980s demonstrates that process of cultural translation which Roger Bromley identifies as characteristic of 'border' writing. Being situated on the boundaries of nations, cultures and classes it achieves its 'very textualisation through constructions of difference and contestations'.[3] This expansion of material is represented by the complex, sprawling format of *The Inner Harbour* which would be echoed in later volumes. Its subdivisions suggest a more discursive thematic range: 'Beginnings' opens with 'Future Work', a satirical comment on the clichéd rejection notes provided by journal editors, the grammatical joke being that it is written entirely in the future tense; 'Endings' contains poems about departures, death and endings of relationships; 'The Thing Itself' concerns her quotidian existence in London. The final section, 'To and Fro', about returning to New Zealand, explores ideas of home and exile. Emma Neale says: 'This shuttling point of view is quintessentially Adcock; the section title emphasises the divided sense of identity she inherits from both family (or historical) emigrant experience and personal expatriation.'[4] This section shows that as her feelings develop about loved ones and family in New Zealand – parents, children, and sister Marilyn – the country and all that it represents continues to serve as an important reference point within diaspora.[5] The mixed surprise and 'trauma' of Adcock's first return in poems of this volume, however, mellow subsequently.[6]

Just as Adcock's earlier volumes chart a readjustment to her youthful mythology of England as the 'true' homeland, *The Inner Harbour* defines the equivalent process in relation to her negative judgement of New Zealand. The same fissured identity and displaced consciousness, the trauma of culture shock experienced upon her previous 'returns' – back to New Zealand in 1947 and back to England in 1963 – emerge.[7] The rhetoric of displacement is tightly controlled, however, as she reconfigures her different attachments and ideas of belonging: to New Zealand with its family ties, to England where her future lies. In 'Instead of an Interview', nationality and the nation state emerge for the first time as traversable boundaries: 'Home, as I explained to a weeping niece, / home is London; and England, Ireland, Europe.' (*Poems*, 115) Significantly these locations are identified with separation from her 'weeping niece', as explanations as to why she cannot stay; the fourfold repetition of 'home' in this stanza underlines the by now familiar conflict of loyalties. But naming 'home' simultaneously introduces the paradox of alienation. No one place constitutes 'nation' or 'home'; nor can Adcock completely shed her old identity, family ties and the previous life which has formed them, symbolized by her 'suitcase full of stones – / of shells and pebbles, pottery, pieces of bark'. These souvenirs of her distant 'home' identify her as different in England. The dual estrangement is apparent in her interpretation of 'exile':

> . . . But another loaded word
> creeps up now to interrogate me.
> By going back to look, after thirteen years
> have I made myself for the first time an exile?

Adcock's uneven habitation of both worlds emphasizes their contrasting prospects. 'Home' in London opens up to the geographical and political categories of England, Ireland and Europe and anticipates her critique of English politics, engagement in social issues and concern for the environment. 'Exile' from New Zealand – despite the prospect of future visits as her parents age and she becomes a grandmother – suggests its marginality as a place of past loss, unfulfilled desire and necessary severance, where

> ... every corner revealed familiar settings
> for the dreams I'd not bothered to remember–
> ingrained; ingrown; incestuous: like the country.

Adcock's 'homing instinct' for England upon her return from New Zealand in 1976, in contrast to that desire for England as the 'lost homeland' which had motivated her return in 1963, demonstrates the fractured subjectivity of the diasporic subject. 'Londoner' begins:

> Scarcely two hours back in the country
> and I'm shopping in East Finchley High Road....
>
> I hardly know myself,
> yet.

(Poems, 116)

This dialogic space in which she renegotiates her hybrid 'British-New Zealand' identity starts with the incongruity of wearing 'jandals –/ or flipflops as people call them here, / where February's winter.' Beyond East Finchley the anonymity of the metropolis is exhilarating:

> ... there across the Thames is County Hall,
> that uninspired stone body, floodlit.
> It makes me laugh. In fact, it makes me sing.

Such double or plural identifications of the subject who lives in diaspora, constitutive of hybrid or interstitial forms of identity, stem from multiple associations and contestations. The flowering of Adcock's verse in the 1980s and 1990s will be severed from any one 'essentialised nativist identity that is affiliated to constructions of nation or homeland',[8] and several new poems in the *Selected Poems* and in *The Incident Book* challenge stereotypes of Englishness and nationality from alternative perspectives.

Other poems in *The Inner Harbour* suggest renewal of and re-engagement with the psychological impasse that Adcock had experienced prior to leaving in 1963: some fragmentation caused by the distancing effects of time and space nevertheless compelled her to reintegrate into the present the forgotten or lost parts of the past – 'the dreams I'd not bothered to remember' – to prevent total erasure. The experience of loss, like that of self-avoidance with which it can be associated, inhibits the desire to go forward.

Adcock's preferred commemorative mode, drawing on mixed emotions – love and fear, happiness and danger – includes returning to past constructions of her psyche. The eponymous poem, 'The Inner Harbour' (*Poems*, 110–111), concerns revisiting the Adcock family boat-shed on the Paremata estuary near Wellington where she and Alistair Campbell first courted. Two subtitles, 'Paua-Shell' and 'Cat's-Eye', refer to local shells while 'lupin-bushes' and 'cutty-grass' which grow on sand-dunes, further identify the locale. The metaphorical overtones of the poem's title – implications of sanctuary and refuge contradicted by the metaphorically unpredictable 'inner' being – are reinforced by the compound-noun subtitles, suggestively imaging the divisions and dualisms of self. That the boat-house is on stilts, that water is below, contradicts the 'wrong belief' of the child in 'The Water Below', refuted when she played below the floorboards of her grandmother's house in Drury. In the final section of 'The Inner Harbour' the narrator, fruitlessly fishing with her shrimping net, enacts what might be read as an adult response to this literal realization of the irrational childhood belief.

The poem invites an allegorical reading with reference to recurring water imagery in Adcock's work: both dangerous and threatening, yet also crucially cleansing, connecting yet trans-formative, it represents the unconscious in its potential to link with the conscious. The empirical observation: 'She is too tall to stand under/ this house. It is a fantasy.' (*Poems*, 111) demarcates the boundaries; that the house allows only immersion in the water recalls 'Over the Edge' whose narrator chooses to swim in the river rather than walk 'barefoot on the gravel'. It also recalls the belief in 'The Water Below' that the water is waiting, that it cannot be easily drained, and the petitions from the Lord's Prayer to ward off its sin and evil. Here, by contrast, the protagonist moves 'further under the shadowy floor', crouches, and finally 'kneels in dark shallow water,/ palms pressed upon shell and weed', apparently choosing to submit to danger. The gesture could be interpreted as a bold re-enactment of Adcock's decision to persist with her 'mistaken' view of the water's presence, and by implication to follow the unreliable impulses of the unconscious. In creating this iconic image of willed movement and stasis (anticipating the act of will in the 'Ex-Queen Among the Astronomers') the poem heralds a reshaping of that framework of desire and victimhood which characterizes Adcock's early poetry concerning male-female relationships.

As well as this re-enactment which compensates for memory's elisions or self-avoidance, Adcock revisits places where she had lived as a child. In 'Going Back', finding her 'own memories tingle' for she had 'left the country /...with certain things undone' (*Poems*, 114), she journeys with her father to find her first school at Tokorangi. This was 'my own most haunting obsession' because there were 'two holes in the map empty' following an earlier nostalgic family tour of the North Island. But her return is fraught with disappointment. They are 'Schools no longer' because subsequently children were sent to city schools; all that remains are 'broken windows, grassy silence,.../ and classrooms turned into barns for storing hay.'[9] Adcock also significantly moves away from nightmares, hallucinations and fevers to patrol more decisively the border between sleeping and waking worlds as in the opening of 'In Focus' where she wakes up with a sharpened realization of the presence of the past. Such poems demonstrate a closer control over the two halves of her psyche as she finds a new inner balance, coming to terms with the past by relocating previously incomplete ideas or ambivalent sentiments within the enlarged world of the present.

THE 'YOU-POEM' AND THE VERSE EPISTLE[10]

Adcock's work remains best known in New Zealand for her conversational voice and informal, colloquial style. 'For Andrew' and 'For a Five-Year-Old' use direct address to establish intimacy, locating the addressee's voice just outside the frame.[11] Personal or 'you-poems' using comment, interlocution or dialogue are a feature of her love poetry as well; but later poems show Adcock developing multiple voices, points of view and different poses. 'The Keepsake', written *in memory of Pete Laver*, demonstrates masterly control of the emotional extremes which constitute its frame: the opening scenario of shared hilarity at unwitting double entendres, detected in the antiquated expression of the advice on courtship in *The Keepsake* (1835), a fashionable anthology, dramatically changes to the singular, distressed realization of the final stanza, where the volume's fly-leaf dedication, '"To Fleur from Pete, on loan perpetual"' (*Poems*, 162), becomes 'a bequest' due to her friend's sudden death. Adcock's restraint appears in the economical accumulation of detail in responses to the book, the stark conclusion which radically undercuts the opening and the delayed release of emotion: 'I've read the lot, trying to get to sleep. / The jokes have all gone flat. I can't stop crying' (*Poems*, 163). Poems written to communicate with family and loved ones in New Zealand show her formal techniques serving specific communicative ends: reinterpreting the past with 'its burden of choices', sustaining relationships, completing half-finished conversations, commemorating friendships, acknowledging influences or saying goodbye. Adcock uses the verse epistle to overcome distance, often as a response to separation, dying and death; but she also parodies and humorously subverts its generic features.

Her first verse epistle, commemorating the death in 1972 of the poet James K. Baxter, blends formal literary allusion with a conversational tone, pointing out that the genre is chosen to match the occasion: 'Dear Jim, I'm using a Shakespearean form/ to write you what I'll call a farewell letter' (*Poems*, 68). Memory works through visualization for 'News of destruction can't delete an image'; recalling 'you, framed in that sepia vision' she makes her own iconic contribution to the Baxter legend; and concludes by re-emphasizing the fit between her form and his content: elegy is the most appropriate genre for one whose 'varied eloquent poems, [were] nearly all / frosted with hints at death' (*Poems*, 69). Adcock's emotions on the occasion of another death, of a lover from cancer, are the subject of several poems. In 'Acris Hiems', writing a letter is her response to 'no good news': 'Friend, I will say in my letter – / since you call me a friend still, / whatever I have been – forgive me' (*Poems*, 75). But this intention is already too late, overtaken by a revelation as sudden and shocking as the news itself: the street with 'the sky white as an ambulance' is transformed into a liminal, half-way place. A van with paraffin for sale 'crawls along', a handbell rings:

> But the painted doors do not open.
> The wind in the ornamental hedges
> rustles. Nobody comes.
> The bell rings. The houses listen.
> Bring out your dead.

(Poems, 75)

Negation and radically shortened sentences sketch this bleak image of death's finality, its ruthless pre-empting of a more prolonged, tender farewell.

But memory, when accessed from a more seductive setting, also offers happier moments. In 'Letter from Highgate Wood', on reading that 'the black invader/has moved into the lymph', she allows the 'green things' of Highgate Wood to work their magic: 'the place won't let me be fearful' (*Poems*, 97). Her recollections become tender, affectionate:

> ...I remember instead
> our own most verdant season.
>
> My dear, after more than a dozen years
> light sings in the leaves of it still.

Characteristically, Adcock juxtaposes contrasting poetic registers and moods at the moment of final reckoning: in 'Poem Ended by a Death' (*Poems*, 97) the opening image of her younger self's distraught address to the deceased beloved is dismissed: 'Fuck that for a cheap / opener'. Instead, drawing on the title's conceit of the relationship as a poem cut short by death, Adcock supersedes the wastage and want that had marked it in real life, presenting an iconic image and new aesthetic drawn from the symmetry and balance between her 'laconic style' and his 'intricate pearled embroideries', which, suggestive of the movement of a verse letter, 'laced us together, plain and purl across the ribs of the world...'.[12]

Other verse epistles mark reunions, as with her sister Marilyn in 1976, after thirteen years. In 'To Marilyn from London', an overview – 'You did London early, at nineteen: / ...And soon enough you were back in Wellington' – marks their long separation and her resignation to the present: 'Somehow you're still there, I'm here' (*Poems*, 116). Their shared choices are embraced – 'Marrying was what we did in those days' – for their balance and continuity. Marilyn's return to England from New Zealand at nineteen is echoed in her daughter Sarah's arrival in England: 'It begins again.' 'Letter to Alistair', addressed to Adcock's ex-husband, Alistair Campbell, is the most explicit of her attempts to reconcile divergent loyalties, disparate geographies and distant nations. Writing from the Lake District Adcock maps the features of its landscape onto the South Island: 'You'd love this place: it's your Central Otago / in English dress – the bony land's the same' (*Poems*, 122). As with 'Tokens' and 'Poem Ended by a Death', language and poetry concentrate the appreciation of the landscape:

> Those thorn trees in your poems, Alistair,
> we have them here. Also the white cauldron,
> the basis of your waterfall. I stare
> at Stock Ghyll Force and can't escape your words.
>
> (*Poems*, 122)

The deictics – 'this', 'those' and 'here' – relativize and coordinate the similarities between the two landscapes. The letter also commemorates and celebrates courtship, marriage, children, family history and activities: Adcock's recent journey to New Zealand, their sons' travel to England, their wedding anniversary: 'Symmetry / pleases me; correspondences and chimes / are not just ornament.' Such parallels, constituting an artistic resolution to the problem of divided loyalties, reiterate Adcock's aesthetic values: 'there must always be layers of meaning, chimes and echoes and unlikely hints of other things to be found on second or third reading'.[13]

More regular trips 'home' diminish the need for this form of address. But Adcock experiments with the dramatic monologue's possibilities for dramatization and the verse epistle's potential for mockery and subversion. Her colloquial voice and conversational style create comical effects as abstract concepts, historical figures and living people all become equally intimate. Prosopopœia or personification introduces mock-confession in 'On the Border': 'Dear posterity' she opens, 'it's 2 a.m. / and I can't sleep for the smothering heat'; the sudden shift of tone and subject matter in the final sentence, spoken in her best mock-absurdist voice, introduces a teasing congruity:

> I am standing here,
> posterity, on the face of the earth,
> letting the breeze blow up my nightdress,
> writing in English, as I do,
> in all this tropical non-silence.
> Now let me tell you about the elephants.

(Poems, 136)

'Villa Isola Bella', equally deflating, was written on visiting the Katherine Mansfield house in the Chemin Fleuri near Menton in 1980 when Marilyn Duckworth held the Katherine Mansfield Memorial Fellowship there. Adcock irreverently revisits the legend – the beloved house ('*You will find Isola Bella in pokerwork on my heart*' runs the poem's epigraph – *Poems*, 139), the wasting illness, the premature death – while also disengaging from it. She announces affinities with her famous literary ancestor: smoking – 'You / smoked shameless Turkish all through your TB. / I drag at Silk Cut filters, duty-free,' – illnesses (real and imagined) and work: 'I brought my tinglings with me, just as you / brought ragged lungs and work you burned to do' – in an imagined late night conversation.[14] Clashes of style and tone undercut them: focussing on bodily functions ('the outside loo', 'pissoir', 'gargle') the language borders on the scatological; negation reinforces the gaps between past and present, herself and Mansfield: 'Your villa, Katherine, but not your room'; Adcock's departure leads her to 'open what was not in fact your door'. There is self-conscious deflation: 'I'm hardly sick at all'. Adcock has hatched 'no maladie exotique' in the Chemin Fleuri, yet her voice projects hypochondria with 'a nameless fever, atavistic fears' as the spectre of her famous forebear's influence looms upon her. The elision between illness and poetic inspiration culminates in the final gesture of detachment: 'Whatever haunts my bloodstream didn't start / below your villa, in our genteel den'. She farewells her crisply, as another sister, not the figure of legend: 'Well, Katherine, Goodnight: / let's try to sleep. I'm switching out the light'.[15]

Like 'Villa Isola Bella', 'The Chiffonier', occasioned by Adcock's mother's bequest of a chiffonier, is a single stanza in rhyming couplets, although its transitions from gratitude, unease, anxiety, affection, to recognition of need, cover more complex emotional territory. Various tones – humorous reflection, anxious and lighthearted speculation, emphatic interjection, solemn affirmation – overlap as it moves between monologue and dialogue. The poem opens *in medias res* – 'You're glad I like the chiffonier'. The belated naming of the addressee reinforces the exclamatory, 'Bless you, mother'. But uneasy gratitude becomes anxiety at her mother's worrying heart condition, making the distance between them 'suddenly swell and grow / from thirty hours' flying to a vast / galactic space between present and past' (*Poems*, 158). Conversation on 'the lighter aspects of your dying' magnifies unease, and her mother's comment – ' "I'll pop off suddenly one night in bed" ' – inspires a snapshot of her as seemingly ageless:

> But now I see you in your Indian skirt
> and casual cornflower-blue linen shirt,
> in the garden, under your feijoa tree,
> looking about as old or young as me.

> (*Poems*, 159)

The realization that opportunities are diminishing – 'How many more times can I hope to come / to Wellington and find you still at home?' – creates an epiphany: the double paradox of writing in her mother's presence to record that the gift will never be a substitute: 'I have to write this now, while you're still here: / I want my mother not her chiffonier' (*Poems*, 159).

BELOW LOUGHRIGG (1979)

'Letter to Alistair' with its links between people, places and poems is one of eleven poems in *Below Loughrigg* which collectively define a spiritual odyssey. Passionate about the hills and valleys of the Lake District and deeply affected by her proximity to the Wordsworths, and therefore to the English romantic verse tradition, Adcock in this volume displays a radiance of being. Falling in love with a place allows her to harmonize conflicting forces and introduces a new dimension of her character, inspired by identification with the 'Wordsworthian' landscape, even recording unexpected symmetries in 'The Spirit of the Place' when 'a deep mad voice bellows

"Wordsworth! Wordsworth!"' (*Poems*, 121). 'Letter to Alistair' shows her earlier problematic relationship with the New Zealand landscape partly propitiated by correlations with that of the Lake District.

Other poems also display a spiritual synchronization between herself and the environment. This new sense of belonging is more pervasive and karmic than the locatedness of earlier London poems, 'Saturday' and 'Trees'. In 'Paths' Adcock proclaims her identification with the Lake District and names herself through identifying its topography: 'I am the dotted lines on the map: / footpaths exist only when they are walked on' (*Poems*, 120). Her fusion of being with the elements acquires an almost mystical aura, recalling Wordsworth of *Lyrical Ballads* or the T.S. Eliot of the *Four Quartets* or, closer to New Zealand, the profundity of one of Colin McCahon's finest paintings 'I AM'. The poem concludes:

> Here on the brow of the world I stop,
> set my stone face to the wind, and turn
> to each wide quarter. I am that I am.

In 'Weathering' the soul's transformation comes from correlating inner perceptions to those of the external world: the semantic density of the title with its overtones of rural life, exposure, endurance and climate change, is matched by the play on 'look' to refer both to her appearance –

> But now that I am in love with a place
> which doesn't care how I look, or if I am happy,
>
> happy is how I look, and that's all.

> (*Poems*, 124)

and to the act of seeing: the 'high pass' seen from the window which 'makes me indifferent to mirrors and to what / my soul may wear over its new complexion'. Such heightened spirituality leads her to identify the place of her soul with the soul of the place, and to wear 'its new complexion' on the 'other' side of her visible self or physical appearance.

Other poems concern acts of seeing, staring, and scrutinizing the natural world, as though experiencing a rebirth. The action of the contemplative gaze in identifying places, animals, insects and birds, or simply appreciating the majesty of the surroundings, is a

recurring topos: 'It is not only the eye that is astonished', begins
'Three Rainbows in One Morning'; 'Binoculars' opens with
'"What are you looking at?"' The extraordinary eponymous
poem, 'Below Loughrigg', sets the scene for this enlargement of
the eye's activity; the first line, 'The power speaks only out of
sleep and blackness', came to Adcock when awakening from a
dream. Written in eight three-line enjambed stanzas and with
only one full stop in the final line, it images rhythms of thought,
movement and coming into being. Describing existence and voice
being created out of darkness – 'The water speaks from the rocks,
the cavern speaks' – it concludes with the arrival of the sun,
bringer of life and light: it 'will not be stopped from visiting / and
the lake exists and the wind sings over it.' (*Poems*, 118)

The concluding poem, 'Going out from Ambleside', also
stresses the immanence of light; this long meditation on living
in Ambleside is presented as the stream of consciousness of an
imaginary, dying hospital patient, old enough to have known
Kurt Schwitters who lived there as a refugee. The penultimate
stanza, reflecting a change of consciousness, opens:

> Dawn light,
> peaks around him, shadowy and familiar,
> tufts of mist over a tarn below.

(Poems, 126)

This and other poems in *Below Loughrigg* display numinously
what 'Letter to Alistair' states explicitly about the diasporic
condition: that the parameters of historical moments in
Adcock's past life have been regrouped into new points of
becoming.

THROUGH TO THE 1980s: *THE INCIDENT BOOK* (1986)

Doublings and repetitions, like those descriptions of the Otago
and Lake District landscapes in 'Letter to Alistair', which
represent some resolution to Adcock's divided loyalties,
pervade later verse. During the 1980s a more syncretic mode
appears in which conflict and oppositions are craftily calibrated
through parallels and 'visual echoes' to create a new centre of
gravity. These poems redirect personal concerns to political and

social issues, creating space for an individual response, as Adcock's distinctively sharp, sardonic style becomes associated with the new discourses of women's liberation and political resistance to Thatcherism. She acquires a more relaxed ironic vision as her outsider position enables her to wittily subvert the constructions of class, gender and region by which the nation defines itself.

Like other diasporic, interstitial writers Adcock at this time began to rethink the rubrics of nationalism; poems such as those in the 'Thatcherland' section of *The Incident Book* sketch minor moments of exile within society; they are modest reimaginings of the relationship between citizen and nation. Overtly sympathetic to minorities and the underprivileged she takes up various causes – the environment, discrimination against women, poverty – but without erasing a centre, for her dualistic vision and outsider's position seemingly correlate with an insider's knowledge of the norm. Mapping the world with the capacity for surprise of a visitor or tourist, she also provides informed insights. Pun, double entendre and 'insider language' with local meanings all contribute to the contesting of the hegemonic values which, from the 1950s to the late 1970s, identified the post-war nation. Titles of poems often carry the weight of this ironic vision. Adcock, now returned from Newcastle, critically revaluates the north-south divide, focussing on the culture of Surrey where she spent some of her childhood. 'England's Glory', a poem about class and regional differences, celebrates the red-tipped matches which the miners of the north use by contrast to the 'safe' matches that bankers use in Surrey (*Poems*, 163); while 'The Genius of Surrey' is 'for the suburban'. Relishing the half-rhyme of 'Surridge' and 'sewerage', the narrator suggests that the industrial north with its dramatic landscapes inspires artists more than the 'rural' monotonous south where 'There had been no industrial revolution':[16]

> Except, of course, the sewerage works,
> on "Surridge Hill", as we used to call it.
> How sweetly rural the name sounds!
> Wordsworth's genius, said Walter Pater,
> would have found its true test
> had he become the poet of Surrey.

(*Poems*, 164)

Poems of the 1980s also demonstrate Adcock shifting her perception of life's oddness from the personal to public events and social change, commenting ironically: the six poems of 'Thatcherland' are miniature snapshots of street scenes depicting the effects of change in East Finchley, the heart of the Prime Minister's constituency. In 'Post Office' recollections of the pensioners queuing at the Post Office door, of familiar landmarks now erased – 'The church was where the supermarket is' (*Poems*, 187) – are counterpointed with observations of similarities in their gestures: the woman who 'swivels her loose lower denture' and the boy chewing gum whose 'jaws rotate with the same motion / as hers: to and fro, to and fro'. 'Demonstration' also ironically contrasts different points of view: addressing 'you', the demonstrator, about the Council's new traffic scheme with 'a monster junction / with traffic-islands, metal railings' (*Poems*, 188), the poem dramatizes the demonstrators losing hope as local issues are superseded by the ambitions of national politics. With a nod to Marvell – 'At our backs / we hear the roar of heavy traffic' – it climaxes with the ringing tones of the Iron Lady herself:

> a stern, conceited female voice
> with artificial vowels exhorts us:
> 'Come with us into the nineties!'

The subject living diasporically acquires an ability to move between divergent viewpoints including that of the excluded or marginalized subject. Adcock renegotiates the boundaries between animal and human worlds, but also investigates the position of old and new minorities in Thatcher's Britain: environmentalists, pensioners, women and children. The perception that identity can be deconstructed or rearranged develops further in *Time-Zones* to the location of in-between spaces or 'interzones', both temporal and geographical, as Adcock continues to challenge hegemonic thinking, and by occupying the margins, begins realigning them with the mainstream.

5

Interrogations: Gender Issues

ADCOCK AND FEMINISM IN THE 1980s

Along with the vexed question of her nationality, gender is *the* centrally defining preoccupation for Adcock. It inspires her most cutting wit and creative powers. Carol Ann Duffy's reference to 'a razor blade in the peach' sums up Adcock's enthusiasm for, yet scathing sharpness about men.[1] But early poems such as 'Incident' and 'Knife-play', which articulate an ambivalence about intimacy and a dangerously compulsive attraction to the role of victim, suggest an experience of identity crisis through relationships in ways that issues of nationhood and belonging can be seen to refract and reflect. Such blurring may reflect Adcock's own era, before the women's question achieved its own form of politicization, when it was spoken for by the discourse of nationalism.[2] She herself notes that the dislocations of place compound and merge with those of gender: 'Wherever I happen to live I have always some residual feeling of being an outsider.' Then asks: 'But now I wonder: has being a woman contributed to this? Are women natural outsiders?'[3] But gender, she claims, has not disadvantaged her in the way that her New Zealand nationality did.[4]

Adcock's handling of gender issues has attracted more critical attention than the issue of her nationality, particularly after the extraordinary decade of the 1980s which saw Thatcherite policies disadvantaging the working class and other minority groups at the time that the sexual revolution became entrenched and women began proclaiming new freedoms for themselves. Adcock came to be associated with public discourses about the role and identity of women and helped to foreground in the public mind issues which had long preoccupied her. She was a somewhat conspicuous figure in the post-Plath sixties and seventies, as she had been earlier in New Zealand, when women poets were, relatively speaking, a novelty; her career has developed in tandem with the emerging public consciousness about women's liberation. Her closest female contemporary is Anne Stevenson and she is often associated with Patricia Beer and Elizabeth Jennings. She gained a reputation in the 1980s for commenting on personal relationships, and for promoting a female consciousness and her work was included in two feminist anthologies: Jeni Couzyn's *Bloodaxe Contemporary Women Poets* and Carol Rumen's anthology of forty-eight poets, *Making for the Open* (both 1985); it culminated in her editing the *Faber Book of Twentieth Century Women's Poetry* (1987).

Whether Adcock was a feminist in the political sense is doubtful; she has spoken out against radical feminism.[5] Coming to feminism as a 'late developer', she is cautious about using the label for poetry: her selection for the *Faber Book of Twentieth Century Women's Poetry* was made principally on the basis of merit although acknowledging the need for 'gendered' anthologies because of women's under-representation in earlier mainstream collections. But radical feminism and the separatist attitude which leads to women's writing being segregated in bookshops under a 'Women's Studies' label alarms her because it seems to prioritize gender.[6] She herself is resistant to being categorized in political, ideological terms: a poem like 'Smokers for Celibacy' that caught the public ear in the 1980s was inspired more by her responses to sex than any public agenda. 'Women's concerns' interest her, but she addresses both sexes:

> I write about things in which women are interested: childbirth, family life, relationships from a woman's point of view, women's histories, women's health, and social questions to do with women. That's what the function of a female poet is. But I don't think you address yourself exclusively to women. That would be to deny half the audience.[7]

Nevertheless, Adcock's growing scepticism about sex and desire, her critique of conventional gender roles and her anti-male sentiments defining a comic, separatist attitude, have made her poetry seem in tune with contemporary feminist agendas. Furthermore, in the 1980s and 1990s she was associated with prominent feminists such as Angela Carter and Lorna Sage who were arguing that women's writing could change public perceptions of women's lives. The emphatic arrival of a new generation of poets like Carol Rumens, Vicki Feaver, Carol Ann Duffy and Jo Shapcott also demonstrated the growth of confidence in and consciousness of women's ability to articulate their needs. Adcock was centrally involved in the euphoric expansion of feminism into a literary movement in the Thatcherite eighties, then, and believed that a woman's tradition, developed through female solidarity, could change the politics of representation. Conversely, the greater understanding of women's issues that feminism initiated led to a more politically aware readership as women increasingly entered public life and issues of sexual inequality, women's victimization, self-empowerment, domestic and public roles, received new attention: her poetry was read by this new audience.

Her gender has dominated Adcock's life and work even before she decided to become a poet: she married, had children, learned to live alone. In fundamental ways at variance from the social norms both in New Zealand and in England she has chosen to exist outside some of the controlling powers of patriarchy, although her predisposition to solitude has meant a certain resistance to any kind of social pigeon-holing. Writing which centres on relations between the sexes, by contrast to writing about nation, home and belonging, reveals a tighter control over the boundary between private and public domains. She retains a degree of anonymity and correspondingly a greater freedom in manoeuvring between conscious and unconscious states. By skilful manipulation of the tropes and conventions of romantic and anti-romantic verse, particularly classical poetry, she projects incidents of personal significance onto the public stage, rendering them accessible without being overtly confessional. Problematic male-female relations have inspired poems about love and sexual encounters which employ the full range of her psychic and emotional talents. Conscious of the subjective disorientations caused by intimacy, she collapses the boundaries between the conscious and unconscious, between dreams and waking states, in ways mimetic of the irrational fears and anxieties that sexuality arouses. Yet she has also used her sardonic wit and dry humour to mock the sexual urges, and has made comic mileage from the mind-body split by questioning the physical, emotional reflexes of desire, introducing cases of mistaken identity as in 'Double-take' and suggesting sexual self-sufficiency in 'anti-erotic' poems, 'Smokers for Celibacy' and 'Against Coupling'.

Andrew Motion sees that Adcock's focus on bed, sex, dreaming, and illness is one whereby she relaxes her self-control, enabling her best writing. 'Her imagination thrives on what threatens her peace of mind, and only when she is unguarded can these threats have their full creative value'.[8] Ian Gregson goes further, arguing that the disordered states, clashes of register and shifts of perspective in poems about gender, as in those about place, are analogues for a general psychological displacement, as 'her personal and poetic identity seem repeatedly in question and her attempts to define it...only increase this feeling'.[9] However such views of the contradictory impulses which inspire Adcock's imagination do not do justice to the significance she attaches to balance and resolution – whether through ironic relativization, nuanced gesture or iconic imaging. Although less dramatic, the processes of resolution and reconciliation are as central to her work as the gamesmanship by which she disorients the reader.

In examining Adcock's ambivalence about gender as a feature of her fractured subjectivity I suggest, contrary to Gregson, that she often defines an equilibrium in male-female relationships; the determined poise of her work is not just aesthetic, it also reflects a desire to establish balance through communication with others. Celebratory poems like 'Composition for Words and Paint', 'Kilmacrenan', 'Glenshane', the retrospective 'A Message' and even 'The Ex-Queen Among the Astronomers', might be read as counterparts to the disorientation that Motion admires when he says: 'she has made a fine art from holding onto principles of orderliness and good clear sense, but she has made an even finer one from loosening her grip on them'.[10] Such 'grounding' poems function in the way that a poem like 'Script' does, in which intimacy with her Drury relatives might be read as reworking the anxieties about the state described in 'The Water Below'. A different form of grounding also appears with Adcock's growing involvement in social issues, her increasing concern for the plight of women – 'Children, little girl children, female protagonists were getting into the poems' – in the 1980s.[11] Drawing on the feminist discourses that align her with writers like Angela Carter, who uses the odd and bizarre to unsettle assumptions about sex and gender, and Lorna Sage who promoted feminist values in lectures, in her autobiography, *Bad Blood*, and in journalism, Adcock interweaves attention to gender with her broadening interest in left-wing politics, community and the environment. Such public attention ensured that women's issues, identified with minority interests, became positioned as part of the opposition to mainstream Thatcherite politics in the 1980s and early 1990s.

ROMANCE, SUBJECTIVITY AND SEXUAL POLITICS

Adcock's earliest poems exhibit a female persona shaped by the pre-Raphaelite, Romantic imagination, who passively reflects a male-defined role as muse or mistress, subject to his desire. In 'Composition for Words and Paint' such modelling of the self upon the other leads to a subjective exploration of intimacy and physical, emotional gratification:

> But you move, and I move towards you
> draw back your head, and I advance.
> I am fixed to the focus of your eyes.
> I share your orbit.

(Poems, 24)

When she began writing in the late 1950s and early 1960s Adcock had no strong female models. She claims she made them up; evidently she was grappling with an insufficient access to representation.[12] Her images of the female as object of male desire and the stereotyped witches, fairies and princesses owe something to her youthful self-romanticizing, but she was also influenced by writers like Edwin Muir and Edna St Vincent Millay.[13] The female subject of her verse is often an *ingénue*, either caught in an undesirable, restrictive role or alternatively liberated, yet inhabiting a hostile, dangerous world; however, Adcock manipulates romantic literary tropes and over-determines the passive female role for ironic effect. A key sequence in *The Eye of the Hurricane*, preserved in *Poems 1960–2000*, sets down parameters of theme and identity: the acquiescent Beauty in

'Beauty Abroad' who goes 'trembling through the gruesome wood' (*Poems*, 17) ('the dewy rose' here an ironic symbol of Beauty's seemingly fatal compact with the Beast), the self-immolating heroine of 'Knife-play', the possessive lover in 'Instructions to Vampires', the disoriented woman of 'Incident'.

'Knife-play', 'Composition for Words and Paint', 'Night-Piece' and 'Afterwards' all explore the emotional risks of intimacy, being marked by an oscillating pattern of attraction and repulsion, of closeness to the lover compounded by an urge to withdraw. The attractions of love, sex and intimacy lead to psychological dislocation, partly shaped by sexual politics, partly by an inadequate process of 'othering'. 'Knife-play' (*Poems*, 18-19) introduces the conceit of the lover as a knife thrower in a circus ring, the narrator, the partner who 'could dance/and dodge...the whistling blades, / turning on a brave performance,' then throw them back. The opening signals the treacherous terrain caused by this symbiosis. 'All my scars are yours,' untrue at the literal level, invokes the bond of brotherhood made by sealing blood on open wounds: 'We talk of pledges'. The slippery possessive pronouns, 'my', 'yours' (from you to me or vice versa? Or shared equally?), destabilize the discourse. Although 'the faint burn on the palm and the hair-thin/razor-marks at wrist and elbow' are 'your tokens' (gifts from you? mementoes of you?), they are self-inflicted, a 'distraction from a more/inaccessible pain'. The hope that this is merely 'a formal test of fitness.../ to bring me ultimately to your regard' is also self-subverting (is your 'regard' of me the same as mine of you?). In this unequal power-game the lover holds all the trumps: 'the long knives...'. The narrator, reversing the teacher-pupil role, gaining the upper hand and mercilessly refusing a truce, enjoys only a Pyrrhic victory; finally both player and game collapse from deeper wounds:

> No, I would make an end of fighting
> and, bleeding as I am from old wounds,
> die like the bee upon a sting.

Female desire is defined on the male's terms: the persona's problematic engagement with him through taking on his identity collapses in on itself. In terms of the poem's guiding metaphor of knife throwing, when 'game' becomes 'real', the performance implodes. The poem's conclusion images this fatal encounter; game-playing fails to empower her despite victory being in her grasp.

In 'Instructions to Vampires' the persona celebrates her sexual powers through possession – warning off a competitor by branding and labelling – rather than through 'Knife-play's' confrontation. She identifies a love triangle using pronouns to delineate ownership and a hierarchy of belonging: 'I would not have you drain / with your sodden lips the flesh that has fed mine' (*Poems*, 19). It concludes threateningly:

> But use acid or flame,
> secretly, to brand or cauterise;
> and on the soft globes of his mortal eyes
> etch my name.

In 'Incident,' however, the impasse of 'Knife-play' recurs as desire is complicated by the terrifying messages of the unconscious. The poem's terse opening with its curt command – ' I came to you / and you said, reaching to take my hand, / "Lie down"' (*Poems*, 19) – establishes an atmosphere of menace, exaggerated by his head '(circled by dead shells)' and the 'grovelling' sea that 'sucked at the rocks and measured the day'. As she falls asleep, dream and nightmare follow: 'a cavernous dream of falling./...a spiral staircase / to hell, furnished with danger and doubt'. The threat that the unconscious registers is realised in the waking perception of imminent danger:

> and you were lying on the grey sand
> waiting for the lapping tide to take me:
> watching, and lighting a cigarette.

(*Poems*, 20)

These three poems, then, define the trajectory of a relationship where mutual attraction is dominated by emotional insecurity – either from reciprocal cruelty, threat from a rival or the disturbing intrusion of the unconscious – all pointing to rejection.

'Night-Piece' hovers on the edge of insecurity, revealing the emotional and cognitive dislocations of intimacy as the dissolving boundaries between human and feral yield a form of synæsthesia, a confusion of the senses.

My eyes open with a click
and meet your eyes, fixed on mine
with steady gaze that licks at my waking face
patiently, like a gentle tongue and clinging
as fur to fingers. Even when I blink
I can hear you watching me.

(TEOH, 34; A. 132)

But it concludes with an image of containment: 'your silent gaze holds me'. Similarly 'Composition for Words and Paint' over-turns sense perceptions in its subjective celebration of a lovers' union. The couple are only forms for,

This darkness has a quality
that poses us in shapes and textures,
one plane behind another,
flatness in depth.

(Poems, 24)

Adcock uses the spatial organization of cubist painting to picture them together as all surfaces ('nothing recedes, all lies extended'). The speaker is disadvantaged by her viewing position, for he is perfect ('You have completeness'), not requiring any frame ('a white line, in delicate brush strokes'), although able to measure others and probe beneath surfaces. She is locked into his movements, puppet-like; but as he is semi-distinct ('Your face; a fur of hair') she can also make him 'materialise' ('your thin wrists, a tooth missing'); and although she may be set on fire ('how I melt and burn before you'), she also finds substance through touch ('My hands prove you solid'). This is a rare poem about the joy of lovemaking, an erotic moment of consummation:

Now I dissolve you in my mouth,
catch in the corners of my throat
the sly taste of your love, sliding
into me, singing;

(Poems, 25)

But it is approached through an aesthetic perception of the other; his existence is no more than what she allows, making him dissolve in the dark. Togetherness, when 'We have swallowed the light', points to relocation within the elements, anticipating the exuberance of happy unions celebrated in other poems like 'Kilmacrenan' and 'Glenshane'.

69

In keeping with the emphasis on myth and fable in this first collection Adcock's male figures are shadowy and insubstantial. The man in 'Incident' is merely an image of enticement or threat and so a foil for her subjectivity. In 'Night-Piece' his 'deep world' is one that she is 'afraid of', yet 'With you I gaze through the close channel/of a telescope at half-predictable stars' (*TEOH*, 33; A. 131). The shadowy, dreamlike settings and anonymous figures in these poems about intimacy suggest the same self-protective instinct that often emerges in Adcock's handling of irony and which can be alienating for the reader;[14] this lies behind the controlling distance of the female presence, and the self-consciously 'located' voice of the woman in relation to the other.

THE FLIGHT FROM ROMANCE

By contrast to these early poems about romantic involvement and being in love, poems about gender written after Adcock's arrival in England are concerned with endings of relationships, with conclusions and affairs which have not taken off or worked out. These are very textually self-aware, displaying the linguistic, verbal adroitness of this period when Adcock is developing the alternative angle on the world reflected in later quixotic, endearing poems like 'Coupling', the mock counterpart to 'Against Coupling', 'An Emblem', a mock-heroic reference to the mating of slugs, or 'The Three-toed Sloth', whose torpor provokes the question, 'What passion ever inspired a sloth to mate?' (*Poems*, 49). Two poems about rejection in love introduce linguistic conceits showing Adcock at her most stingingly acerbic. 'Parting Is Such Sweet Sorrow', as the pointedly sarcastic title suggests, deals with the verbal banalities which mark the end of an affair. The narrator is bedazzled by them, imaging the clichés as mechanized yet flashy, brittle and potentially wounding:

> Words
> glitter in colours like those gaudy prints [of tropical birds]
> the speech of a computer, metal-based
> but feathered like a cloud of darts.

(*Poems*, 27)

Appropriating her rejected lover's 'signal-system' she 'mints' her own debased, de-romanticized phrases: ' "I am in your hands; I throw myself upon / your mercy...'''', and so empowered literally dematerializes him:

> I lift you like a bale of hay,
> open the window wide, and toss you out;
> and gales of laughter whirl you far away.

Adcock's fine economy with figurative language, often used to create an atmosphere, reinforce a point or strike a pose, here extends beyond that of 'Knife-play' by making metaphor function as verbal weapon; the culminating satiric image further challenges expectations as language overtakes 'reality'. The explicitly savage 'Advice to a Discarded Lover' which follows 'Parting is Such Sweet Sorrow' has been praised for being organized 'as skilfully as any fine, neat seventeenth-century conceit'.[15] Imaging 'our dead affair' as the decaying corpse of a bird, it wittily contrasts the formal lecture tone of 'Think, now' with cruelly candid observations like 'In you / I see maggots close to the surface. / You are eaten up by self-pity' (*Poems*, 29). Commenting that skeletons are less offensive than putrefaction, the speaker chillingly dismisses her suitor: 'Do not ask me for charity now: / go away until your bones are clean.'

The changes brought about by platonic friendships instead of sexual relationships are the subject of 'Afterwards', introduced through the rhetoric of superstition and obsession. The couple is possessed by a 'thing' which is unhealthy, addictive, draining:

> We weave haunted circles about each other,
> advance and retreat in turn, like witch-doctors
> before a fetish.

> (*Poems*, 40)

The ambiguous phrasing of 'But love, this ritual will / exhaust us' (direct address or the noun 'love'?), combines with the speaker's insinuating tone of danger. The cosily confiding voice – 'Come closer' – conveys the very treachery which her words disavow: 'this gentle talk, with no pause for suspicion, / no hesitation'. The narrator counsels a new ritual: not recognizing or naming 'the thing', for loss of cognition is required for this reduced empire of the senses: 'A nothingness, a non-related-ness, this / unknowing into which we are sliding now / together'. The poem concludes with a seeming gesture of submission, but the facile tone of the word 'gentle' once more suggests menace: 'Rain is falling. Listen to the gentle rain'.

The control required to translate the decision in favour of physical denial into a new balance between self and other underpins the magnificent achievement of 'Kilpeck' (*Poems*, 71). Written after visiting a church in Herefordshire famous for its Celtic carvings, 'Kilpeck' registers the verbal and gestural nuances of an exploratory relationship. The poem's setting locates the overt sexuality of the historical iconography – 'serpents writhing up the doorposts' and the shelagh, the Whore of Kilpeck, 'holding her pink stony cleft agape' – in conscious contradiction of their deliberate decision to avoid 'the sweet obvious act' which is marked by the speaker's reflection: 'We have our reward'. The male voice hints that poetry might now channel such energies: 'Last night you asked me / if poetry was the most important thing'. The poem celebrates their tentative equilibrium – 'We are dried and brittle this morning, / fragile with continence, quiet' – as if a newly acquired physical state, as they slither down a slippery track, holding hands 'to keep a necessary balance'. Yet a hint of sterility, even emptiness, in this posture is implied: 'A fruitful county. / We regard it uneasily'. The apprehension of transience and mortality pervading the poem culminates in the conclusion: the unchanging postures of the gargoyles whose 'feral faces' are 'less lined than ours', are contrasted to the carefully negotiated movements and 'burden / of choices' of the two poets whose identities are threatened by the passing of time.[16]

In poems written in the late 1970s Adcock is poised between recollection of the headier romantic impulses of 'those wild-garlicky days' (*Poems*, 97) which created turmoil and confusion, and the arrival at decisions which confirm the more desirable (by now) state of self-sufficiency. This flight from romance demands assessment of its place among other choices and possibilities. 'Folie à Deux', like 'Afterwards' and 'Kilpeck', about avoidance and alternative rituals, represents togetherness as 'pica', a perverted craving for unpalatable foods: 'acorns ...and moonlit roses – / perfumed lettuce, rather unpleasant:/ we rinsed them from our teeth with wine' (*Poems*, 73). The speaker attributes their 'shared perversion' to him – 'you were the one / who nibbled the chrysanthemums' – in seemingly not discriminating between the sacred and the profane: 'You speak of ceremony, / of something to celebrate'. By contrast church bells make her 'fear blasphemy' (*Poems*, 74). Adcock blurs the boundaries between rituals: one is 'postponed' and replaced by another, sitting 'face to face' and talking, yet even as 'that fey couple' who

> ... lay
>
> manic with words,
> fingers twined in each other's hair
> (no closer) wasting nights and hours;

and who 'chewed, as dry placebos, / those bitter seeds and flowers', sexual consummation is doubtful. The slowly paced final stanza with its opening and closing half-lines images the momentousness of their choice – 'We rise, and touch at last' – reinforcing the connotations of sacrifice in 'fasting' and 'sacrament'.

'Folie à Deux' is a study in ambiguity between the religious and secular, the sacred and the profane. Its hints of abnormality invite interpretations of heterosexual relationships as disturbing some natural harmony. The poem as artefact projects the working-out of the lovers' dilemma: 'It is the moment' demarcates a new future, one which will be dominated by the 'sacrament'. The precisely measured tones, the ordering of detail, the short phrases and brief sentences, represent stylistically the couple's difficulty in arriving at their decision. But the longer cadenced sentences of stanzas six to eight describing the two types of lovers and their rituals, acquire momentum, as if sealing off the past with its message of continuity from the present with its demand for sacrifice.

The contrast between the passionate past and the austere present is the basis for some playful poems in *The Inner Harbour*. The volatile onset of frenzied passion in 'Prelude', mimicked through rhythms and sound patterns, suggests imminent consummation: the 'erotic' long dry grass with 'hair-fine fronds of straw' and 'feathery flourishes of seed' invites them:

> to cling together, fall, roll into it
> blind and gasping, smothered by stalks and hair,
> pollen and each other's tongues hot on our faces?

> (*Poems*, 88)

The conclusion teasingly deflates this fantasy: 'We walk a yard apart.... We have known each other, remotely, for nineteen years'.[17] 'Accidental', an ironic counterpoint to 'Folie à Deux', ruefully acknowledges that sexual desire can overwhelm the civilizing restraints of friendship: accidental passion is scathingly dismissed as 'this blind unstoppable robot walk / into a conspiracy of our bodies' (*Poems*, 89). But in 'A Message', which follows, the accidental event is seen as one of those botanical mutations which provoke belief in a larger, Darwinian scheme of things: 'Let time tell'. The speaker, writing a letter to a former lover, concludes by withholding any conclusion, but the final injunction includes the general reader with the addressee:

> Gardens are rife with sermon fodder. I delve
> among blossoming accidents for their designs
> but make no statement. Read between these lines.

(*Poems*, 90)

The metaphysical dimension of 'A Message' helps 'relocate' romantic love within philosophical, biological contexts.

Poems written about endings of relationships, however, show Adcock at her most dryly secular and verbally austere, using her 'laconic style'. The six line 'Tokens' is about the absence of the lover. The poem is a medium linking the lovers; it registers the affair as a symbiosis of sex and creativity: 'your forgotten pipe and tobacco, / your books open on my table' has a peculiar, enduring efficacy: the lovers' 'joint essence' – of which 'the sheets have been laundered' – is volatile still, because 'a compound, / not a mixture' and hence capable of further change; and the poignant presence of the beloved remains as 'your voice speaking in my poems' (*Poems*, 77).[18] Love's endurance through the poem as artefact in 'Tokens' contrasts with the uncompromising tone of 'Send-off', a terse, four-liner which astringently delineates an airport farewell. He brings 'what was left of our future together: two drinks on a tray' (*Poems*, 95). It is paralleled and extended by 'Poem Ended by a Death', an emotional obituary which introduces her imagined youthful self torn by grief and concludes with an elegantly defined image of remembered harmony, reinforced through mutual admiration of each other's writing (*Poems*, 97).[19]

WOMEN OF MYTH, LEGEND AND THE CONTEMPORARY

In poems written in the 1980s Adcock's public voice is at its most stridently political. She speaks out against the social conservatism of Thatcherism and, increasingly involved in gender issues, pronounces on women's inequality and victimization, poverty, ill-health and the environment. Her poetry shows mobile and plural constructions of the self and other, a more densely negotiated sense of identity with a myriad of reference points. After two decades of living in diaspora Adcock has accommodated that other great tension in her verse, the conflict of loyalties between two countries; her ability to twin dual allegiances or relativize conflicting viewpoints appears in a more flexible handling of perspective. There are no longer the starkly decentred, disempowered female subjects of the poetry of the early 1960s. Feminist discourses had opened up new possibilities of representation for women by the 1980s, a decade when Adcock reached 50; putting romantic illusion behind her and weighing up the value of relationships against her desire for solitude, she moves adroitly between competing points of view. For example, the long poem 'Soho Hospital for Women' shows her as ironically detached, sympathetically involved, registering the familiar as though it is strange, but also reaffirming the normal. Her style and approach become more relaxed, urbane and allusive and she develops a talent for imitating voices.

Adcock's affirmation of new possibilities for women through inventing more powerful, extravagant images of the female, begins with her own sense of expanding horizons, celebrated in the opening poem of *The Inner Harbour*. 'Future Work' imagines an explosion of her creativity simultaneously as novelist, playwright, as translator of Persian creation myths, the pre-Socratics and Lucretius, as chess champion and:

> Yes, there will certainly be poems:
> they sing in my head, they tingle along my nerves.
> It is all magnificently about to begin.
>
> *(Poems, 84)*

Correspondingly, her earlier ambivalence about heterosexual relations is redirected into a flamboyant celebration of womanhood, carving out new territory by contrast to earlier poems about enigmatic or unusual men such as 'Clarence Whatmough' or 'The Famous Traitor'. 'The Ex-Queen Among the Astronomers', a triumphant statement of female self-possession, has provoked controversy among male critics who argue that its exaggeration of conventional gender roles and sharp divisions of power (men being associated with scientific exploration, women with erotic gratification), reinscribe female passivity and patriarchal control;[20] or alternatively that it interrogates patriarchal patterns of meaning indirectly by disrupting fixed subject positions.[21] The Ex-Queen is presented as male-dependent: 'she walks as she was taught to walk / for his approval', implying non-liberation and exile; but her assertion of desire in the last two stanzas suggests self-empowerment approaching transcendence:

> She plucks this one or that among
> the astronomers, and is become
> his canopy, his occultation;
> she sucks at a earlobe, penis, tongue
>
> mouthing the tubes of flesh; her hair
> crackles, her eyes are comet-sparks.
> She brings the distant briefly close
> above his dreamy abstract stare.

(Poems, 93)

This act of sexual pleasuring suggests an alternative source of power to science with its mechanizing effects upon its servants. As the astronomers' 'occultation' who reduces distance, the Ex-Queen with her crackling electrical hair and comet-spark eyes supersedes the voyeuristic desires and optical illusions of the myopic scientists who 'serve revolving saucer eyes,/... wait upon huge lenses... carry pocket telescopes / to spy through' and cherish 'little glassy worlds'.

The belief that scientific discourses are outstripped by organic, internal powers is one to which Adcock devotes her most imaginative resources. Nor is this specifically gendered; the Ex-Queen's gift for transformation recalls the fable-like poem, 'The Man Who X-Rayed an Orange'. A man who makes an orange levitate believes he has failed in not creating 'a perfectly imaginary orange' to replace the real one (*Poems*, 23). His explanations – 'mysticism, occult physics, /alchemy, the

Qabalah' – are dismissed: 'If there was failure, it was only here / in the talking.' The poem's magisterial conclusion, using *litotes* and *occupatio* to mark his singular achievement, parallels the Ex-Queen resplendent in the appeasement of her carnal appetite:

> For surely he had lacked nothing,
> neither power nor insight nor imagination,
> when he knelt alone in his room, seeing before him
> suspended in the air that golden globe,
> visible and transparent, light-filled:
> his only fruit from the Tree of Life.

(Poems, 23)

In 'Mary Magdalene and the Birds' Adcock celebrates the biblical figure's legendary reputation as a prostitute, her ability to don different disguises – 'I switch voices, adapt my features' (*Poems*, 145) – and hints at her innate compassion. In ventriloquizing Mary Magdalene's multiple birdsong voices lifted in song, as 'all birds to all men', she shows her as truly protean in a way that matches Irigaray's idea of woman's essential fluidity:

> Woman is neither open nor closed. She is indefinite, in-finite, form is never complete in her ... This incompleteness in her form, allows her continually to become something else, though this is not to say that she is ever univocally nothing. No metaphor completes her.[22]

Interweaving Mary's other role as Christ's chief mourner, '*With my body I thee worship*', imaged as a rock-dove 'cold on that bare nest/...unlulled', the narrator in the final stanza 'corrects' those women who heard her song as 'a swansong'; instead its sounds are those of near-fatal seduction:

> ...the spring curlew
> or a dawn sky full of larks,
> watery trillings you could drown in.

(Poems, 146)

As Adcock intervenes in patriarchal constructions of posterity, expanding her repertoire to include fictional recreations of the life-stories of women in legend and history, she uses ventriloquism. 'On the Land' mimics an anonymous voice from the Great War: that iconic figure, the landgirl, 'in my puttees and boots and breeches / and a round hat like a felt halo' (*Poems*, 177). The poem's narrative allegorizes the battlefield *in extremis*: the unexplained pain 'that wouldn't stop' that she suffers in the fields leaving her 'doubled up' suggests the death-throe agonies of soldiers on the killing fields of Flanders and Gallipoli. Images of decapitation and death in her grubbing for potatoes at harvest-time, 'mining for stray':

> ... Round segments
>
> chopped clean off by the blade
> flashed white as severed kneecaps.

(*Poems*, 178)

– the whole ones are 'baby skulls' – harden into a more explicit parallel with wounding and maiming suggested by her collapse into a trench and after rescue, her tossing and writhing on the hard bed. Adcock's preference for hard edged realism means that such suggestive synchronizations are unstrained: both realistic and allegorical readings are possible. The landgirl's collapse may have been due to a miscarriage given the poem's naturalistic opening, but its hermeneutical richness lies in the hint of a more general interpretation.

A more extended act of ventriloquism occurs in 'Mrs Fraser's Frenzy', a five part poem which charts the decline into incurable madness of Mrs Fraser after her enslavement by aborigines. Written as songs for music, it introduces different voices adopted from different versions of this famous legend, recording the controversy and confusion surrounding her capture. Eliza Fraser, the wife of the captain of the *Stirling Castle*, shipwrecked off the Queensland coast in 1836, lived among an aboriginal tribe as a wet-nurse to their children until she was rescued. As a rare captivity legend in which the colonial encounter is reversed, and familiar from Patrick White's novel *Leaves of Grass* (1976) and Sidney Nolan's paintings (1947-64), it has become a founding myth of Australian nationhood.

Adcock converts nineteenth-century interpretations of this event – of native barbarity, savagery and the debasement of European civilization – into a study of female derangement. Mrs Fraser was excluded both from the indigene's wild zone where she was held captive ('put among the children' (*Poems*, 219)) and then, after being rescued, from her own society. Exceptionally she ventriloquizes the voices of Mrs Fraser's captors, the 'colonized' aborigines, to emphasize the epistemological gulf separating them in this doomed cultural encounter; they call her a 'white she-ghost' who 'had forgotten our language' and 'wouldn't learn' to 'collect food, to dig for roots' (*Poems*, 218). Eliza Fraser's descriptions of 'savages', 'cannibals', 'abominable monsters' with bright blue hair growing in 'tufts / on the tips of their shoulders' draws from accounts which sensationalized her story (*Poems*, 217, 220).[23]

Mrs Fraser's obsessive repetition of her name hints at the unhinging of her mind due to her loss of husband and child and her degrading treatment. Her attempts after returning to civilization to 'prove' her story, in all its contradictions, are challenged by a masculine European-Australian voice which rejects her fantastic claims to have been dispossessed and her demands for material compensation. A further perspective comes from her second husband, Captain Greene, who sees 'a strangeness in her, gone beyond the strangeness / of anything he'd met on the seven seas' (*Poems*, 220). The irreversible changes to her identity as Eliza Fraser culminate in the poem's most extreme image of disintegration: into a sideshow freak. Eliza's lament at being robbed of 'civilisation: clothes, possessions / decency, liberty, my name', and the terrifying psychological chasm that this has opened up –

> There can never be
> enough of anything in the world,
> money or goods, to keep me warm
> and fed and clothed and safe and free.
>
> (*Poems*, 221)

reinforces her traumatic spiral into loss and non-being, making her Adcock's most radical example of female alienation.

Adcock's compassion for women who have suffered from neglect, illness or maltreatment or who are victims of male predatoriness or social mishap, in particular environmental disaster, is interwoven with an acute sense of their individuality. 'The Soho Hospital For Women' registers the alienation of internment:

> Strange room, from this angle . . .
> strange bed, mechanical hum, white lights.

There will be stranger rooms to come.

(Poems, 101)

Medical science – 'the gloved hands and the speculum' – is also defamiliarized by an allusion to the mythological Hine-Nui-te-Po, the castrating Maori goddess of death. Sharp visual observations create portraits of cancer patients on the ward and their attitudes to the disease: Doris who 'has to pin the slack waistband / more tightly over her scarlet sweater' each week; 'Mrs Golding / who never smiles. And why should she?' (Poems, 102). Her own survival and joy on being discharged to 'stand...giddy with freedom, not with pain' and 'move to the checkout, to the rain, / to the lights and the long street curving' (Poems, 103), by no means diminish this empathy, but rather offer a new perspective.

In the sombre poem, 'Witnesses' (Poems, 189), allusions to women of myth and legend dramatize the highly charged atmosphere of the 'black-clad proceedings' of a court room drama in which a child's fate is at stake; imaging the witnesses as Macbeth's three witches 'crouched over the only / ashtray, smoke floating into our hair' and the defendant in the witness box, Adcock's friend whose suitability as a mother is in question, as Joan of Arc, 'straight, still, her neck slender, / her lips moving from time to time', she graphically represents the inequality of such trials. Hints at masculine salaciousness underlie accusations of 'these ferretings under her sober / dress, under our skirts and dresses / to sniff out corruption'. The heavy hand of patriarchy is visualized in the cluster of bewigged, dark-suited men intimidating the defendant into frozen immobilization. Ellipses – pauses, hints, hesitations – imply the deviousness of the judiciary system as the judge intones in favour of her husband: '"that you yourself initiated the violence.../ that your hysteria..."'. Adcock leaves the reader in suspense, demanding that such detail be interpreted as an indirect attack on discrimination against women.

'Witnesses' examines complex social attitudes whereby victimhood is reinforced by the very legal structures which are apparently intended to protect it. In poems about male predators recalling Adcock's 'victim' stage, primal fears underlie the cautionary voice. Two poems of the early 1980s, possibly

80

inspired by the sensational attacks of the Yorkshire Ripper, recall 'Bogyman': 'Across the Moor' examines the disturbed mind of a stalker who lets his victim go because 'she was not the one' (*Poems*, 142). 'Street Song' invokes the scary tactics of male predators through creepy movements:

> someone is loitering in the dark,
> feeling the giggles rise in his throat
> and fingering something under his coat.

(Poems, 141)

Reciting a list of Newcastle street names in the jaunty rhythms of a child's nursery rhyme, Adcock concludes on a warning note.

> So don't go lightly along Darn Crook
> because the Ripper's been brought to book.
> Wear flat shoes, and be ready to run:
> remember, sisters, there's more than one.

(Poems, 142)

Adcock moves away from her earlier autobiographical explorations of relationships in these decades; her decision to remain unattached is one source of her absurdist take on gender which attuned her to the more sexually explicit mood in women's writing of the 1980s. By contrast to the earlier finely-tuned heroines prone to nightmare or dream and chaotic perceptions of self and other, she now ironically appreciates the unreliability of existence as a cause for surprise. In 'Accidents' she registers unpredictability by over-determining the common condition of ignoring the tricks of fate:

> The accidents are never happening:
> they are too imaginable to be true....
> The rescue party digging all night in the dunes
> can't believe the tunnel has really collapsed:

(Poems, 177)

As aware of female impulsiveness as she is of predatory intent, Adcock sidesteps the treacherous unconscious with its potential for disaster. The old preoccupations and fears recur in more benign contexts; although residual traumas remain, conscious recognitions put irrational fear on the borders of the text. 'Crab' (*Poems*, 135) can be read allegorically. The narrator,

81

seen as wanting in decorum, avoids a desired yet inappropriate intimacy, imaged as eating 'the permitted parts of the crab'. These obstacles are part of the poem's coming into conscious-ness: the couple 'wrench open' the crab suggesting the danger of sudden betrayal by the body: 'flesh bursts out of its cup'. The crude act of instant gratification, reminiscent of sexual con-summation, is implied by the speaker's wrongful temptation to eat 'The dark fronds' called 'Poison...Dead Men's Fingers' – just as the hasty indiscriminateness of passion tempts one to desire the 'wrong' parts (because not on offer) of the other. The parallel is made explicit through simile: 'you snatch them from me, as you snatch / yourself, gently, if I come too close.' The apparent moral, 'we are safe again in words' testifies to the narrator's newly acquired 'appropriate' detachment; yet the final line, 'All day the kitchen will smell of sea', evokes the elements and feelings which the couple have avoided, so undermining this poise. In a poem whose semiotics – of gesture and movement – are so powerfully suggestive, language itself comes to play a crowning role in unsettling any fixed position.

Poems in the 'Incidentals' section of *The Incident Book* which demonstrate a pronounced rejection of men, hostility towards masculine power yet susceptibility to its attractions, are leavened by an absurd-fantastic streak. The same mind–body conflict that occurs in 'Crab' and 'Afterwards' reappears in the comic, shifting perspectives of 'Double–take' (*Poems*, 183), a poem whose linguistic structures enact (and mock) the narrator's quandary. Startled that her next-door neighbour resembles her ex-lover in being paunchy and balding, the narrator reminds herself that only the mundane features of her ex-lover's personality now interest her. The poem develops the conflict between her desire for detachment and her body's compulsive attraction to him. The ordinariness of both men enables her to turn herself off; the same language about them in stanzas one and three which conclude: 'you are relieved / to find that you don't fancy him', seemingly collapses them into one, yet the appearance of linguistic control is as superficial as her own unreliable recognitions. Is mock-fancying the neighbour a rehearsal for remeeting her ex-lover ('a week later...at a party')? Just when she thinks she is immune, her body tells her otherwise: 'Why are your legs prancing / so cheerfully along the pavement?' The poem's 'epiphany' – 'You go home cursing chemistry' – recognizes those unconscious yet intuitive instincts which the anti-male strategy of her textualizing self would deny.

How to deflect female desire and channel it through other sources (and discourses) is the focus of Adcock's famous 'anti-erotic' or anti-masculinist poems. Anti-romantic irreverence about men which recalls anti-feminist writers like John Skelton and the Goliardic poets of the twelfth century, Hugh Primas and the 'Archpoet', whose works she translated, converts denial into satirical entertainment. 'Against Coupling' (*Poems*, 49–50), later a cult poem and described as 'the wittiest and perhaps the sanest poem ever written in praise of masturbation', anticipates the mood of the women's revolution.[24] Heterosexual love becomes repetitive to the point of boredom 'when / one feels like the lady in Leeds who / had seen the *Sound of Music* eighty-six times'. Laying down the gauntlet 'in praise of the solitary act', the mock-pulpit voice recommends readers to 'embrace it without/ encumbrance' because 'Five minutes of solitude are enough'.

'Smokers for Celibacy', written more than twenty years later in the same preachy tones, mimics a pro-smoking manifesto: 'Some of us are a little tired of hearing that cigarettes kill'; it recommends 'what you should give up is not smoking but sex' (*Poems*, 215). The pompous, self-righteous voice is comically magnified by the information-packed, over-extended lines of some couplets. Listing unsavoury diseases 'generously spread around by men's cocks', it welcomes cigarettes as cylindrical substitutes. Paradoxically a masculine presence is reinscribed through this phallic imagery for, albeit sanitized and de-eroticized, the orally induced satisfaction cigarettes provide can be read as analogous to the sexual act. The poem's humour comes from this potent analogy and its comic 'performance' of sexual relations through reconstruction:

> [Cigarettes] aren't moody; they don't go in for sexual harassment and threats,
> or worry about their performance as compared with that of other cigarettes,
>
> nor do they keep you awake all night telling you the story of their life,

beginning with their mother and going on until morning about their first wife.

(Poems, 216)

The need for choice in sexual matters is also at the heart of 'Excavations' (*Poems*, 181), a witty 'excavation' of past lovers imaged as incarcerated in holes in the ground. This 'Dantesque scenario' is partly about settling old scores; the narrator throws earth on those who give excuses for abandoning their women, ' "I went off you, / or I was frightened, or my wife was pregnant, / or I found I preferred men instead" '; but another kind of justice prevails; those 'men whom I stopped loving / and didn't tell...' have the contented existence she might envy, 'cuddled up with their subsequent ladies'. Neither category creates a viable match and the humour masks the narrator's isolation. 'Choices' (*Poems*, 184) develops further this compromised attitude to heterosexuality: men needlessly complicate women's lives with their boring conversation, needs, desires, and less than attractive bodies. The prospect of life alone on a desert island reinforces the exclusionary mood of 'Smokers for Celibacy'; yet even here with a 'sea-and-sun-proof crate of cigarettes', revelling in the fact that there is 'nobody, thank God, to lecture you / on how he managed to give them up', men remain conceptually at least, an ineradicable part of existence. Just to prove that singular isolation is only one perspective, 'Kissing' offers a serenade to the ubiquitousness of sexual attraction. As a way of life which spreads from the young who've 'got all day' to the middle aged who 'are kissing / in the backs of taxis, on the way to airports and stations' – kissing overcomes the treachery of time: 'They too may have futures' (*Poems*,182)

Gender issues dominate Adcock's entire work and extend to relationships that are not defined by either heterosexuality or female celibacy; many friendships are recorded with sensitivity and tact, family relationships, especially in her role as a grandmother, elicit tender and affectionate sentiments. From these perspectives Adcock's anti-erotic poems occupy an extreme position in the emotional spectrum, one of spirited denial without necessarily meaning an unambiguous rejection. Gestures of repugnance or disdain are always compromised by an instinctive attraction, and her best poems like 'Double-take' work through an implicit acknowledgement of this contradiction.

The oscillation between desire and restraint underpins the comedy of her famous dream-poem: 'A Political Kiss' (*Poems*, 262), about kissing John Prescott. Self-sufficiency in Adcock's case matters not because men are impossible but because relationships themselves require too great an effort at adjustment and repositioning. Men have always been a crucial presence in Adcock's life but the effort of sustaining a balance in heterosexual relationships has increasingly yielded to that greater imperative: of maintaining more than one position simultaneously within the slippery territory she encompasses in her poetry.

6

Creatures, Journeys,
Eco-Politics

Adcock's heightened ability to resolve conflict and relativize differences in poems written in the 1980s and 1990s, evidence of a more dialogic, reconciliatory mode, is manifested through a rehandling of earlier themes – creatures, travel and journeys – and the introduction of new concerns such as the state of the environment. *Time-Zones* (1991) exhibits the fluidly mobile diasporic subject whose multi-locational attachments enable transitions between different points of view, traversal of the boundaries between different species, states of being and cultures, and the creation of hybrid identities.[1] New spaces are registered, familiar ones are revisited and revised from more global perspectives: poems about eco-politics embracing issues concerning the environment and climate change, poems about journeys, represented by air travel and the transitions between time-zones, coexist with those about her life in East Finchley. Adcock's perception about social attitudes to disability and disease is sharpened while her increased consciousness of mortality and the vulnerability of all species emphasizes the precariousness of the boundary between life and death.

CREATURES OF DREAM AND THE EVERYDAY

Adcock's passion for the natural world (*Poems*, 279), and observations about the habits of creatures have inspired some of her most original perceptions – the caterpillar, for example, is seen as 'that moistly munching hoop of innocent green' (*Poems*, 88) – and her most popular poems.[2] In early poems dream and

86

nightmare produce distortions of nature. The title of her second volume, *Tigers*, aptly captures the feline elegance, intensity and sharpness of her own style; but feral animals were then also a part of her interior world, appearing in dreams and intruding into her waking life as fevered manifestations of her unconscious. In 'The Pangolin' she asks: 'Why do I dream of such large, hot-blooded beasts / covered with sweating fur and full of passions?' (*Poems*, 32). In 'I Ride on My High Bicycle', by contrast, the surreal vision of an animal in the landscape appears as a seamless fusion of dream with reality.

> Now it is very early morning
> and from my window I see a leopard
> tall as a horse, majestic and kindly,
> padding over the fallen snow.
>
> (*Poems*, 27)

The apparently normal spectacle of that implausible combination – a genial leopard, horse-high in snow – demands the reader accept the presence of the absurd in the everyday. Such striking dislocations of the 'real' create a fabulist world in which the relationship between animals and humans is deliberately skewed. 'Think Before You Shoot' conveys an upside-down world of children wielding guns against tigers invading their wood and tigers who exact reprisals upon children. But this dreamlike state of affairs belies a moral outlook. The narrator's question, 'Will you prefer the death / of prowling stripes to a mush of trampled stalks?' (*Poems*, 31), reverses the saying that tigers will eat naughty children. The know-it-all adult voice does not explode the fable; but the conclusion raises issues about the morality of killing 'tigers' in 'their wood' by suggesting the superior logic of animals when threatened by humans: 'They want you, / and it's no excuse to say you are only children./ No one is on your side. What will you do?' (*Poems*, 31)

Adcock's ability to see the animal world in terms of the human world becomes a potent source of her comical, lop-sided vision in later poems and she lightheartedly redraws the boundaries between them. Such deliberate disordering of reality can be seen as metonymic of the diasporic subject's geographical displacement and relocation through acquiring new subjectivities: interrogations of her own identity enable deconstructions and reconstructions of other types. Like Angela Carter's rewritings of fairy tales, her subversive poems offer insights into scientific taxonomies. In 'Tadpoles', dedicated to her first grandson Oliver, she whimsically collapses the boundaries between animal and human to make a point about likenesses between the embryonic origins of different species. Examining a glass bowl of tadpoles about to turn into frogs, she imagines herself as one of them: 'Taddies, accept me as your grandmother,/a hugely gloating grand-maternal frog' (*Poems*, 159). But observing the differences between the species in growth-rates and transformation she then deconstructs this imagined likeness:

And Oliver lay lodged in his dreamy sphere,
a pink tadpole, a promise of limbs and language,
while my avatars of infancy grew up
into ribbon-tailed blackcurrants, fluttery smooth,
and then into soaked brown raisins, a little venous,
with touches of transparency at the sides
where limbs minutely hinted at themselves.

(*Poems*, 160)

The renegotiation of identity within a liminal and dialogic space extends to an interest in the bodily construction of humans and animals, their reproductive organs and modes of procreation. 'Gas' is a surreal vision of a society which is regularly visited by gas, 'dealing out death or duplication' (*Poems*, 56). For survivors, 'Division, not union, is the way we / must reproduce now', as clones are replicated so that two, four, even eight versions of the same person appear. This paradoxical state of celibate togetherness – 'There is no sex now, when / each has his undeniable partner' – develops into a futuristic scenario in which desire and the erotic are effaced:

.... How lust
for what is utterly familiar?
How place an auto-erotic hand on
a thigh which matches one's own?...

(*Poems*, 55)

Although thinking of 'one's identical other' elicits no human curiosity or sexual desire in 'Gas', elsewhere the opposite is apparently true. Pairing involves mirroring and the matching of one creature to another. Adcock picks out the bizarre and unusual mode of coupling with a naturalist's eye. In 'An Emblem' the twinning of slugs as they mate, indistinguishable from each other, making first a horseshoe then a circle 'tail to snout', presents a perfect emblem of 'heraldic serpents coiled in a twist':

> The ends link up: it's a shiny quoit
> of rippling slug-flesh, thick as a snake,
> liquorice-black against the white
> paint: a pair of wetly-nak-
> ed tubes.

(Poems, 137)

In 'Coupling', an amusing riposte to 'Against Coupling', she observes the way that one crane-fly can jump start another and apparently vice versa: 'They do it tail to tail, like Volkswagens:/ their engines must be in their rears' (*Poems*, 204). Such 'naturalistic' poems confirm assumptions about the human mode of reproduction which 'Gas' satirizes, that mating is about mirroring or seeking an identical version of oneself. The sceptical view that coupling involves neither desire for joining nor negotiation of difference but merely replication underpins the anti-masculinist sentiments of 'Against Coupling' and 'Smokers for Celibacy' – a source of humour as well as wonderment. Its logical conclusion is manifested in perhaps her most unusual poem, 'Last Song', in which displacement is comprehensive as the biological, ecological orders which validate mating are overturned. In this vision of an indescribable post-apocalyptic existence Adcock farewells the principles of doubling, matching and balance by which every species, animal and human, is constructed, and their formal aesthetic of symmetry:

> Goodbye, sweet symmetry. Goodbye, sweet world
> of mirror-images and matching halves,
> where animals usually have four legs
> and people nearly always two;
> where birds and bats and butterflies and bees
> have balanced wings, and even flies
> can fly straight if they try.

(Poems, 190)

Adcock's alternative world 'when this one's gone skew-whiff', when humans will revert to the very ecological elements

89

from which they have sprung, is one which she has already entered by imagining herself as elemental matter in poems like 'Foreigner', 'Downstream' and 'Happiness' (*Poems*, 107, 128–29, 204). 'Last Song' displays further dissociation from normality than the earlier 'Regression' where 'All the flowers have gone back into the ground' (*Poems*, 26); 'Regression' asks 'how shall we endure as we deserve to be?' 'Last Song', if any answer, is an ominous one, for both human beings and animals have decomposed into 'algae or lichen' in a world where 'If the flounder still exists it will be king.' Adcock's vision here reaches out to the post-human condition at its most radical and post-cultural.

The frailty and vulnerability of wildlife and creatures is a new focus of *Time-Zones*, contrasting with the earlier monstrous beasts of dream and nightmare. The subject matter – her street in East Finchley, her backyard and neighbours – and the stress on sight and sound represent a narrowing of focus from the local community of 'Thatcherland' in *The Incident Book*. It anticipates the even closer focus on the particular and the emphasis on touch – by way of communicating beyond the grave – which runs through the 'ancestor' poems of *Looking Back*. *Time-Zones* is dedicated to 'the memory of my father, Cyril John Adcock, 1904–1987', and Adcock's layered emotional responses to his death are most poignant in her poems about nature.

'Toads' makes clear that mourning her father leads Adcock to discern pathos in the vulnerability of the natural world; the dying toad might be a leitmotiv for his death:

> It was the summer of my father's death.
> I saw his spirit in every visiting creature,
> in every small thing at risk from harm:
> bird, moth, butterfly, beetle,
> the black rabbit lolloping along concrete,
> lost in suburbia; and our toad.

> (*Poems*, 196)

Adcock's affection for the species appears in her embrace of the dying toad: '... it lay lengthwise / flabby-skinned across my palm,/ cold and stiff as the Devil's penis' (*Poems*, 197). The mini-resurrection when 'a little shadow shaped like a brown leaf/

hopped out of greener leaves and came to me' comes almost as relief from mourning and she joyfully cradles the 'reborn toad': 'a gently throbbing handful – calm, comely, / its feet tickling my palm like soft bees.' In this reckoning plants and creatures acquire not merely anthropomorphic potential, they signify an alternative eschatalogical reality.

Other poems revise earlier associative processes, such as the wavering line between waking/ conscious and dreaming/ unconscious states. The opening of 'Wren Song' – 'How can I prove to you / that we've got wrens in the garden?' (*Poems*, 198) – reaffirms the stronger call of 'authentic' reality above that of her unconscious. Although she is asleep:

> I can hear him, . . .
>
>> his bubbling sequences,
>> an octave higher than a blackbird's,
>> trickling silver seeds into my ears.

This is not a dream. By contrast her desire to get up to record the song, apparently a logical continuation of her enjoyment, is. The poem's 'proof' is in disallowing any other medium, including her unconscious will to agency, to intrude between what she hears and external reality: 'it was a dream, the getting up./ But the wren's no dream. It *is* a wren.' (*Poems*, 199) Movement and sound traverse the barriers separating one location from another, here the garden from the bedroom; the wren's 'piccolo solo' accompanying his 'sprints of zippy flight' is symptomatic of inter-zonal movement, like that of the toad who 'returns' from the dead and the despised dandelion in 'Under the Lawn' which when uprooted leads to buried treasure: 'an octagonal threepence, a George the Fifth / penny and . . . rusted solid, Grandpa's scissors, the ones for hairdressing' (*Poems*, 198). 'Heliopsis Scabra', by contrast, paints an ominous picture of impending death in August, 'the time of year when people die', symbolized by the survival of:

> . . . these daisy-faced things
> [which] blare like small suns on their swaying hedge
> of leaves, yellow as terror.

> (*Poems*, 200)

91

The daisies' tentacular clutch on life which makes 'other plants /
less greedily rooted...at risk' illustrates Darwinian selection
and nature's indifference: 'The sky surges and sulks. It will let
them die.'

The resistances to death recorded in 'Heliopsis Scabra' are
matched by the renewals of 'House-martins' when the drought
breaks. Here Adcock rewrites her themes of dispossession and
loss in human affairs, self-consciously abandoning the reassur-
ing correspondences that anthropomorphism offers, instead
placing human emotion under the microscope, dramatizing the
play of time in the construction of memory. The poem's
opening, 'Mud in their beaks, the house-martins are happy...'
(*Poems*, 200), leads to an enquiry once the seductions of art are
disposed of: 'of human children it's permissible / to say they're
happy – if indeed they are'. The question of happiness becomes
the centrepiece of a childhood scene which is reconstructed
with the same deliberation as the camera unrolling in 'In Focus'.
The same exact delineation of time with transitions from the
present into the future appear when – 'in fifty years or so':

> Arrange to present them with...

> a blackbird's song, the honeyed reek of privet,
> and a flock of house-martins, wheeling and scrambling
> about a group of fake-half-timbered semis.

> Call it a Theme Park, if you like:
> 'Suburban childhood, late 1980s'
> (or 70s, or 50s–it's hardly changed).

(Poems, 201)

Happiness becomes that less 'authentic' sentiment, 'nostalgia',
when the present, now the past, is reassessed by the children,
now adults, who despite the fake architecture of the mock-
Tudor cul-de-sac, are heirs to sentimentality: 'Ask them "Were
you happy in Shakespeare Close?" / and watch them gulp, sick
with nostalgia for it.' Adcock's scepticism about the myth of
home is nowhere more apparent than in this deracinated vision
of British suburbia. Stan Smith notes: 'These suburbs of
unauthenticity are the site of the real. Such originary places
are always confidence tricks in which we connive at being taken
in, made to feel at home, the more poignantly to savour our
dispossession.'[3]

JOURNEYS, ECO-POLITICS AND THE ENVIRONMENT

In the 1980s the alternating pattern of Adcock's life was well established: regular journeys – to New Zealand, to Adelaide as Writer in Residence in 1986, and to Romania – interrupt her settled London life. The hyphenated title, *Time-Zones*, suggests the coordination of the temporal distinctions of 'zones' as periods of time with the dynamic of spatialized time-zones as experienced in travelling.[4] Transitions between the hemispheres and the different time frames of distanced locations, the subject of poems like 'Central Time', 'The Breakfast Programme', 'Meeting the Comet', are represented as stylistic coordinates. Use of tense and point of view suggests the tension between different places in 'My Father' as she registers her absence when he died ('he went to it so suddenly,/... with both his daughters so far away' – *Poems*, 195), recalling her earlier maxim about farewelling her son: 'No one can be in two places at once' (*Poems*, 44) and another poem about her father, 'Cattle in Mist'. Such transitions which recognize 'distal' origins (Manchester and Wellington) bring into focus the more recent 'points of origin' in poems about 'proximal' relationships in East Finchley, like 'Toads', 'Under the Lawn', 'House-martins', 'Next Door'.

Time-Zones also demonstrates Adcock's concern for the environment and the future of the planet, hinted at in 'Last Song', due to the increased dangers of chemicals, pesticides, pollution, and global warming. Her environmental consciousness merges with a magnified sense of how the odd embraces the normal, sharpening her public satiric voice. While 'domestic' poems focus on the mortality of different species, 'global' poems utilize international settings: the airport lounge and customs officials of 'Meeting the Comet' and 'Aluminium' are in-between spaces epitomizing the transience of the traveller. Longer poems which rewrite legends or fables or which are protest songs, using sub-divisions, multiple voices and conflicting viewpoints, show her imaginative, narrative powers extending into these new territories: 'Mrs Fraser's Frenzy', 'The Farm' and 'Meeting the Comet' all reflect the new concern with mortality with their themes of madness, disability, disease, and death. Nations and nationhood are now figured in relation to eco-politics as the impact of environmental disasters or policies is traced in poems like 'The Greenhouse Effect' (set in Wellington) and 'The Farm' (set in England), rather than to issues of origins and belonging.

The major themes of diaspora – return, home and exile –, therefore, are reconfigured as Adcock, in the decade following her father's death, sees herself less in terms of conflicting diversity than in reconciling differences and overcoming distances. This is apparent in her ironic mockery of the local versus the global in 'The Breakfast Programme', written from Adelaide where 'chemical weapons, radioactive rain' are seen as 'one of those messy bits of northern gloom / from the places where gloom's made (not here, not here!)' (*Poems*, 208). In the journey to New Zealand (and back to England) in 'Meeting the Comet' she rewrites her own 'to and fro' trajectory as narrative-fable. This also redefines the genre of the 'travelogue' poem, as unexpected satirical insights emerge from the themes of disability and abnormality at its core. The idea that the world's 'gone skew-whiff' returns as the fictional traveller, living with her own birth defect, perceives tourists in ways that redefine freakishness: 'The tour guide rounds them up: his travelling freak-show' (*Poems*, 225). In poems about elusive female ancestors in *Looking Back* such reconciliations extend to a belief in the spirit's immortality.

Adcock's positions on environmental change, the threat to ecology, the survival of the planet, are articulated through a satirical discourse and subversive point of view. The new battle line between man and the environment is redrawn by the comic, post-apocalyptic voice of 'From the Demolition Zone' with its image of humanity at war requiring literature as salvation: 'Come, literature, and salve our wounds:/ bring dressings, antibiotics, morphine; /bring syringes, oxygen, plasma' (*Poems*, 209). The deadening effects of the political situation of Romania variously insinuated in 'On the Way to the Castle' culminate in the final chilling image of peasants fossicking for potatoes with 'the size and consistency of bullets' (*Poems*, 211). Middle-class values are satirized in 'A Hymn to Friendship' and Adcock remains knowingly yet unrepentantly subversive of political correctness in the celebrated 'Smokers for Celibacy'.

Adcock's exploration of borderline states between living, dying and death, between disability, malformation and health, between different species types, even between neighbours, as in 'Next Door' (*Poems*, 199) shows her as increasingly 'at home' in her multiple, in-between environments, because alive to the oddness of existence. Two poems set in New Zealand relate concerns about environmental damage to the southern hemisphere where the ozone layer began to disappear in the 1980s: 'The Greenhouse Effect' discusses the effects of global warming observed as a 'fizzing light on the harbour' and as nature disordered: 'Aerial water, submarine light' (*Poems*, 204). The apparently romantic observation – 'Wellington's gone Wordsworthian again' – is corrected: Wordsworth would have 'admired' it but disapproved 'if he'd heard / about fossil fuels, and aerosols,/ and what we've done to the ozone layer'; while the conclusion – 'Just for now, I can live with it' – (*Poems*, 205); reflects anxiety about the uncertain future. 'The Last Moa' concerns rumoured sightings of this now extinct giant bird. Only seen in museums now, the moa's 'sad affronted mummified head/...is as old as a Pharoah' (*Poems*, 205). Adcock illuminates the misconceptions in our knowledge of the past using *occupatio*:

> Somewhere in the bush, the last moa
> is not still lingering in some hidden valley.
> She is not stretching her swanlike neck...
> for a high cluster of miro berries,
> or grubbing up fern roots with her beak.

She makes these locations substitutes for the moa's absence. Past species' genocide as a foretaste of present-day indiscriminate consumerism, is implied by the cannibalistic innuendo of the repeated 'gobble':

> Our predecessors hunted and ate her,
> gobbled her up: as we'd have done
> in their place; as we're gobbling the world.

> (*Poems*, 206)

The moa is gendered as female. Other women who are accidental victims are the tragic heroine of 'Mrs Fraser's Frenzy' and Fiona Lodge who died of leukaemia after a radiation leak in the Windscale disaster in the 1950s. 'The Farm', dedicated to Fiona's memory, laconically contrasts the 'rough, authentic rural charm' of the farm to the hidden lethal danger. Written in loosely rhyming couplets, the pauses created by gapped half-lines suggest growing horror as the full implications of the disaster emerge. Adcock's collective, doom-laden voice emerges in the concluding half-lines which mock-pedantically spell out the worst, a cancer invasion:

> Before long most of us will know
> people who've died in a similar way.
> We're not aware of it today,
>   and nor are they,

(*Poems*, 212)

The long, three part cosmic fantasy, 'Meeting the Comet', uses flight and space travel to explore and redefine the category of disability. The young heroine's right arm and hand are malformed due to her mother's unknowing exposure to aerosol insectides during pregnancy. She travels from England to New Zealand in 1986 to see Halley's Comet whose rarity makes it a fitting objective correlative to her condition: '"I'm not the only one, but I'm once / in a lifetime."' (*Poems*, 226) The poem concludes with her 'choiring' of the stars in a new 'harmony of the spheres', an '*Instrumentalis...Humana*' – and in a Chagall-like elevation, like the comet, gliding 'off the edge of the star-chart' (*Poems*, 228). 'Aluminium' also involves air travel and introduces cosmic imagery: 'a ring of sky' and 'an aerial hum'. Adcock's moralizing, state-of-the-nation voice proclaims 'here's awful Alzheimer's looming again' (*Poems*, 213) and poses the impossible choice of impure water, 'bacteria soup' or 'sinister granules'. A grim warning 'of dementia to come', due to the Water Board's premature decision to use aluminium as a water purifier, concludes the poem.

Poems published in the second half of *Looking Back* and in the 'New Poems' of *Poems 1960-2000*, extend some of these concerns: 'Summer in Bucharest' is a poem in code which uses summer fruits as ciphers to represent different political factions in Romania at a time of intrigue, rumour and innuendo: 'raspberries are discredited', 'strawberries are seriously compromised' and gooseberries have 'been infiltrated / by raspberries in gooseberry jackets.' (*Poems*, 266) 'Libya', about the American bombing of Libya in 1991, returns to the theme of family generations which the last two publications explore further: Adcock's grandchildren, subject of 'Trio' and 'A Visiting Angel' (*Poems*, 269, 274), and other children whose anti-social instincts are captured in humorous incidents such as 'The Video'. Unlike these more lighthearted snapshots of family scenes or encounters, 'Libya' presents the terrifying prospect of apocalypse through a mixture of political and domestic registers: the narrator's wryly parenthetical comments, reviving cold war anxieties about nuclear explosion, sharpen the implications of the television news which the adults are watching:

> When the Americans were bombing Libya
> (that time when it looked as if this was it at last,
> the match in the petrol tank which will flare sooner or later,
> and the whole lot was about to go up)

> > (*Poems*, 193)

Amidst mounting chaos in the living room, the children's cries represent another response: ' "I'm too young to die", "I don't want to die"; while the baby who 'banging her spoon sang "Three blind mice, three blind mice" ', provides an even more astringent comment than the adults' anxieties on the myopia of American foreign policy.

Adcock's more extended habitation of diasporic space apparent in poetry written after her father's death shows the 'genealogies of dispersion' becoming inevitably intricated with those of 'staying put' as she rewrites her ideas of home in multiple contexts.[5] Her 'homing desire', rather than her 'desire for a homeland', however, is most powerfully manifested in her wish for proximity to her ancestors; in *Looking Back* she aims to restore continuity to the disrupted cultural and ancestral heritage which migration to New Zealand represented by intervening in the processes of history, recovering the voices of her forebears and reconstructing their stories.

97

7

Seeking the Ancestors

Adcock's most recent volume, *Looking Back* (1997), contains twenty-four poems about her paternal ancestors inspired by discoveries made through genealogical research. Although her fascination with her ancestors first emerges in poems in *The Scenic Route* about her mother's family from Northern Ireland, including those who migrated to New Zealand, it was catalyzed into a search for them by her father's death in 1987. Since then she has reconstructed in prose her family history beginning with her father's life in Manchester and ending with her childhood in New Zealand and England.[1] In verse she has invented the stories about specific ancestors, identified by name, feature or life event, and animated by her discoveries of photographs, gravestones, houses and other relics. The whole process can be seen as marking that compulsive need to define her position.

In terms of diaspora theory and of Adcock's unusual paradigm of being doubly exiled, this obsession can be read as a version of the diasporic subject's mystical search for origins due to the hunger for knowledge about and intimacy with an archaic idea of 'home'. This imagining of original absolutes is one consequence of the white settler's reduced authenticity or authority within the nation state.[2] Adcock's desire for 'symbolic ancestral reconnection' as a response to rootlessness or dislocation was renewed and strengthened in response to her father's death.[3] By then she had already explored in verse that process of cross-cultural referencing between New Zealand and England, which according to Homi Bhabha is an 'ambiguous movement of transit that lacks any celebratory closure'.[4] The return to the historical past, also a return to her poetic roots through ancestral reconnection, is a similar movement of translation. It can be interpreted as a direct response to colonization, a desire to remedy the disruption and loss caused by migration, to restore continuity to the broken line of descent by reconnecting the umbilical cord with the mother country.[5] Re-establishing these links on genealogical and ethnic grounds is made not just to 'prove her English credentials';[6] it represents a culmination of Adcock's lifelong project of exploring and traversing the boundaries of nation, time and space.

THE COLONIAL HERITAGE

Adcock's desire to locate her ancestors first appears in 'Please Identify Yourself', a poem written upon first visiting Northern Ireland, then factionalized along religious lines. Her own allegiances, by contrast, are approximations only: 'British, more or less; Anglican, of a kind' (*Poems*, 61). The poem introduces a different uncertainty: she could not find the graves of 'my tough Presbyterian ancestors, / Brooks and Hamilton', in Cookstown and Moneymore 'among so many unlabelled bones'. She overcomes this loss with an affectionate gesture: 'I embrace you also my dears'. Although the title 'Please Identify Yourself' evokes the surveillance methods used in that IRA era, it is also an appellation, a Gramscian calling into existence, to which Adcock's figurative encompassing of her lost ancestors is a preliminary response. Two other poems in *The Scenic Route* are complimentary cameo portraits of her maternal great-grandparents, Richey Brooks and Martha Hamilton, focussing on their migration to New Zealand, and like the later poem, 'Settlers', dwelling on the hardships of the journey out and the pioneering life. 'Richey' (*Poems*, 62) is about Richey Brooks who migrated from Moneymore to Drury in 1874. The mud which dominates his origins (Moneymore was '"a place of mud and nothing else"'), subsequent life and death – in Drury he found 'mud again –/ slipped in the duck-run at ninety-three' – links the two hemispheres and their landscapes. 'The Voyage Out' focuses on Richey's wife, Martha's sea journey with her four children: newly pregnant with her fifth she trades half her dietary ration for 'extra lime juice from the crew' (*Poems*, 62).[7] This colonial voyage is 'not the middle passage, no', but yet risky and uncomfortable:

But who could envy Martha? Sick
with salt meat; thirsty; and gazing on
a sky huge as the whole Atlantic,
storm-waves like Slieve Gallion,
and no more Ireland than went with her.

(*Poems*, 63).

These poems complete the process imaged by the metaphorical embrace in 'Please Identify Yourself'. The Drury / Londonderry trajectory of Richey's life has been reversed in Adcock's visit to Northern Ireland; her 'return' can be seen as a counterpart to their migration 'out', completing the loop they have initiated.[8]

With them belongs 'Settlers' which recreates the voice of Adcock's paternal grandmother, Eva Adcock (*née* Eggington), recalling the voyage from Manchester in June 1914 with her husband, Sam, and son, Cyril (Adcock's father, later called John), their early life in New Zealand – 'she and the boy much alone' – her return visit to England with Sam in 1932–3, and her final 'retraction into a city' (*Poems*, 112). It records a visit Adcock and Marilyn made to their grandmother in Wellington when she was alone in the house and suffering from Alzheimers. The fractured, fragmented style, unusual for a poet so strongly attracted to the order of syntax and grammar, dramatizes her grandmother's disconnection from her mind and wandering memory.[9] Lack of punctuation, gaps suggestive of pauses or sentence breaks, uneven stanzas and intermittent rhyme, image the breaks caused by the process of emigration, separation and departure, described as 'all their people fallen away / shrunken into framed wedding groups'. The blurring of the narrator's voice with Eva's through the narrative technique of free indirect speech in lines 1-6 dramatizes the difficulty in recovering shreds of her story. The visit itself – 'We took her a cake for her birthday' – deepens into sympathy for her grandmother, whose delusions are projected through disordered syntax:

wondering she must have been why
alone in the house or whether alone
her son in Europe   but someone
a man she thought in the locked room
where her things were stored

(*Poems*, 113)

100

Eva's voice comments on family photographs: 'Them's your Grandpa's people' and the narrator compassionately sums up, 'Much neglected' (at being left alone in the house): 'and much here omitted   Footnotes'. Eva's halting recall of departure in 1914 is confused with the arrival in New Zealand, while the narrator's reference to 'the whole slow long knotted tangle' sums up the complicated family affairs, and possibly her own decisions in the light of family history. The conclusion again dramatizes the overlapping voices: youthful Eva is seen, possibly by her husband-to-be, Sam: 'And her fine straight profile too/ her giggle   Eee   her dark eyes'.

Adcock's determination to uncover her ancestors' lives and write her family history came after the sudden death of her father in 1987. In 'My Father' the decision is linked to the desire to bring him back, to overcome the finality of death, as repetition, equivalences of line and syntax, and precise rhythms confirm.

> I'll go to look for where they were born and bred.
> I'll go next month; we'll both go, I and my sister.
> We'll tell him about it, when he stops being dead.
>
> *(Poems,* 195)

Ironically, when this news arrived, Adcock was visiting Manchester, his birthplace and home until the age of ten. The confusion at not being able to find the places where he lived becomes an objective correlative of her distress and sense of loss. The suburb of Hulme – ' "a rubbled / wasteland, a walled-off dereliction /...It's nowhere now"' (*Poems,* 194) – is surrounded by other gaps and dead-ends suggestive of non-existence: 'Hulme and Medlock. A quarter of a mile / to nowhere, to the names of some nothing streets'. Paradoxically these streets and suburbs where her father and his family once lived had been 'beatified in my family history file'. Her own grief –'Even from here it catches in my throat' – coincides with puzzling over the street plan of Manchester, 'checking the index, magnifying the net / of close-meshed streets in M2 and M1.' (*Poems,* 195) Disjointed half rhymes, sentence-breaks juxtaposed against line-breaks and abrupt half-line sentences concluding stanzas two, four and six, image the disorientation caused by the sudden loss, now indelibly linked to the

misleading cartography. But the final stanza opens with a
swelling momentum of enjambed lines as the intention to search
for the ancestors and unlock the silence of the past is
resoundingly announced:

> There must be roads that I can walk along
> and know they walked there, even if their houses
> have vanished like the cobble-stones – that throng
>
> of Adcocks, Eggingtons, Joynsons, Lamberts, Listers.

LOOKING BACK: FINDING THE ANCESTORS

Adcock's poems about her father's forebears are presented in
reverse chronological order starting with two about Sam Adcock
and Eva Eggington who migrated to New Zealand from
Manchester and ending with one about a sixteenth-century
ancestor, 'Peter Wentworth in Heaven'. Although each poem
focuses on a family member or members, the portraits are also
shaped with reference to their place in the family tree: 'Nellie (*i.m.*
Nellie Eggington 1894–1913)' (*Poems*, 237) is about one of Eva
Eggington's sisters who died from TB which she caught at the
mill; Nellie's prolonged illness delayed the plans of Eva, Sam and
Cyril to migrate to New Zealand. The speaker in 'Amelia' says: 'In
'72 my brother hanged himself' (*Poems*, 241). This tragedy appears
in 'Samuel Joynson', about a restless, unhappy character searching
for an unnamed, unknown thing, perhaps happiness; as a final
solipsistic act 'he tied a noose where it should have been / and
slipped his head into it, for one last look.' (*Poems*, 241)

The creation of these ancestors demonstrates Adcock's gift for
invention through ventriloquism and dramatic incident, as well
as her technical mastery over diverse genres and modes: the
sonnet, ballad, quatrains, tercets, narrative poems. Through
monologue, dialogue and other narrative techniques she
converts genealogy into drama, imparting to history the energy
of a living quest. She is the literal signpost to the past, the
reader's tour guide, with her camera

> ballooning out like a wind-sock
> from my wrist, showing the direction
> of something that's blowing down our century.

(Poems, 234)

The opening poem, 'Where they Lived', introduces an historical moment and place: 'That's where they lived in the 1890s.' It argues that uncovering the secrets of the past and exposing family skeletons is the descendants' prerogative:

> They don't know that we know,
> or that we're standing here, in possession
> of some really quite intimate information
> about the causes of their deaths,

(Poems, 234)

'Framed', which follows, invokes the Victorian technique of cameo portraiture, making the poem a leitmotif for the sequence. Likewise Adcock's questions about her paternal grandparents, which 'frame' this poem, announce her personal quest: 'What shall we do with Grandpa, in his silver / frame?' Curiosity about gender inequality prompts her to ask: 'Why not Grandma, still shyly veiled in her / tissue paper and photographer's cardboard?/... Why did he not frame her?' (*Poems*, 234). Sam and Eva's wedding photo, dated 1 September 1903, is the subject of '227 Peel Green Road': both families are lined up outside the Eggington family home in Manchester. Past and present are elided as the point of view shuttles between the figures in the frame and the surviving Victorian features of the house. Adcock uses *occupatio*:

> Failing their flesh and bones we have the gatepost.
> Failing the bride in her ostrich-feathered hat,
> the groom bracing his shoulders for the camera,
> we have the garden wall, the path, and the gatepost:

(Poems, 236)

Adcock also resurrects her female ancestors, drawing attention to women's earlier anonymity in the public sphere. Using first-person narrators and a range of verse forms, she ventriloquizes the voices of three ancestors, focussing on their fates. Each poem articulates a moral encomium and records a gift to posterity in a 'memorialising' moment. In 'Mary Derry', a three-part poem in unrhymed couplets, an unwanted pregnancy, a hasty marriage, then infant death ('You knew he died? The wages of sin' – *Poems*, 239), are conversationally recounted. The climax – 'Then I died' – includes a posthumous comment on the long shadow of consumption stretching over four generations.

'Amelia', written in two fourteen-line stanzas, opens *in medias res*: 'It went like this.' (*Poems*, 241) Family tragedies – the deaths of two children, the suicide of her brother – pushed her to gin, leaving her dead 'of a stroke, officially; "of drink" / wasn't spoken aloud for forty years'. The split between her two selves appears in her portrait – 'an old thing in a shawl, with a huge nose' – and a photograph – 'a maiden / with frightened eyes and a nose as trim as theirs.' The conundrum is her children's: 'I couldn't have been both, they're sure.' The memorial of 'Frances', by contrast, foregrounds the struggle over property and bequest. About the two marriages of Frances Weale, it quotes from her will of 1638: '*Item I give to my sonne Samuell Browne / my halfe dozen of silver spoones...*' (*Poems*, 248) – as evidence of how she controlled her destiny. Frances defied the will of her first husband who 'was going to rule us all from beyond the grave' (*Poems*, 249) by marrying the guardian of her second son, appointed by her husband (who had also left him the spoons): so 'I kept both my children'. The narrator imparts symbolic value to her signature: 'The wobbling / jabs of the quill are hers, an image / of weakness spelling out her strength' (*Poems*, 250), a familiar motif to Adcock who has boldly shaped her own life by writing.

Elsewhere Adcock offsets the anonymity of death with a symbolist technique, creating an iconic image. The illness of 'Barber' ('sounds like cancer'), recorded as dying after fifteen months of 'spinal disease' at the age of 20, already qualified as '"Hairdresser (Master)"', is imaged through the tools of his trade: the very knives he wielded so proficiently become the blades of the illness slicing through him:

It felt like blades

burning, slicing — a whole year
to play the Little Mermaid, walking
on knife-edges, with hand-glass and comb.

(*Poems*, 242)

In 'Sub Sepibus' another nameless ancestor is recorded for her misdeed as the epigraph taken from the parish register for Syston, Leicestershire in 1667 explains: those married clandestinely were excommunicated. Yet the woman's lighthearted, ballad-like song chiming as a 'refrain' on 'Tommy Toon', her lover's name, subverts this censorious sentiment: 'Under a hedge was good enough for us,/ my Tommy Toon and me' (*Poems*, 245).

Poems where the narrator interacts with ancestors through empathetic identification, re-enacting or mythologizing her desire to create them, are the most compelling. The sonnet 'Water' describes an encounter with a nameless water-carrying ancestor. Their passing becomes a moment of recognition as the ancestor's expression, the coldness of the water, the roughness of her clothing, and her smell are all palpable.

> I stepped aside as she trudged past me,
> frowning with effort, shivering slightly
> (an icy drop splashed my foot too).
> The dress that brushed against me was rough.
> She didn't smell the way I smell:
> I tasted the grease and smoke in her hair.
>
> (*Poems*, 243)

Image-making occurs through sense perception: the sonnet concludes by exposing the illusion – 'No, I didn't see her. But she was there' – as Adcock challenges the reader with the textual evidence. Significantly the poem's only enjambed line occurs at mid-point with physical contact between them when water from the ancestor's bucket splashes onto the narrator's foot. The distance and intimacy between self and other is finely judged, making the poem's form represent matching but separate images of 'relations', joined at just this one point.

'A Haunting' with its physical tussle and swift verbal exchange goes to the opposite extreme: '"Hoy". A hand hooks me into a doorway' (*Poems*, 243). Displaying the grotesquerie of Magwitch of *Great Expectations* this figure is the most fully developed of Adcock's gallery of threatening predators: unruly, unkempt, shadowed by the past with the diminished stature of the pre-modern: 'Eyes in a smudged face. Dark clothes. A hat..../...A stunted stump of a man', this unsavoury character with 'too many aitches' triumphantly subverts any romance about ancestry being sacrosanct: '"Look at me! I'm your ancestor."' Needling and scornful with 'a snaggle of teeth (predentistry)' (*Poems*, 244), he exploits the family connection – '"Give us a kiss!"' – taunting her with '"I'm what you dug"'. His historic presence is deflated in turn. The narrator breaks the illusion as she throws him her purse full of pound coins, what is 'base metal to him, proleptic wealth, no use / for more than a century to come.'

Just as the arrival of an unruly ancestor unsettles any complacency about ancestor hunting, so ideology and politics are undermined by the past. Adcock uses her favourite trope of retrogression to show how returning to the past is atavistic, throwing up cruder sentiments. The opening confession of indifference to politics in 'The Wars' (*Poems*, 244) contrasts with the concluding evidence of financial inducement to follow military matters. The Gulf War of 1991 drives the narrator 'to the 18th century./ 'I could see no glory in this life' and so 'When...they offered us the Recession instead / I went back further'. Her search, which ignores contemporary affairs, is contradicted by the final line which invokes the questionable ideology of heroism and self-sacrifice that she has turned her back on. The bequest to John, brother of Edward Russell, is for '"ten pounds by the yeare / to be paid him soe long as he followes the warrs..."' (*Poems*, 245).

More self-reflexively autobiographical are poems about female ancestors whose elusiveness encourages renewed efforts to reconnect through psychological disinterment. In 'Anne Welby' (*Poems*, 246) the place and date of her death – '9 May 1770, Beeby' – appear in the epigraph; but Anne's burial ground in the churchyard is not discoverable. The narrator questions the viability of her passion: 'what did I want to do after all – / burrow into the earth and stroke her skull?' Although the bare facts alone are given on the stone's inscription, genealogical research sustains the emotional charge that kinship promises; it encourages a sense of propriety and propinquity, enabling the sensation of physical contact to blur into a sense of physical presence:

> As I stroke the stone
> with hands related to hers, I can feel
> the charge transmitted through eight steps
> of generations. She's at my finger-tips.

> (*Poems*, 247)

The vital connection to her female forebears that 'Anne Welby' signals unfurls in 'Beanfield' which even more assuredly overcomes the gap of centuries separating her from another ancestor, Frances St John (the great, great-grandmother of Anne Welby). Adcock is realistic about the limits of her pursuit:

> Somehow you've driven fifty miles to stand
> in a beanfield, on the bumpy ridges
> at the edge of it, not among the blossom
> but under the larks –

(Poems, 247)

The house, ploughed into the earth, is no longer visible but the certainty that this is Frances – 'She's here; she's not here; she was once' – is reinforced by the larks, unseen but heard: for 'they...left the twitter of larks,/ a pins-and-needles aerial tingling'. Descent and lineage are properties of birds as well and the sonnet concludes on a cosmic note: 'The larks are other larks' descendants./ Four hundred years. It feels like a kind of love.' The transcendence of the affections in this poem constitutes a high point; for the lack of any surviving traces of Frances St John, topographical or otherwise, other than through bird song, is compensated for by a spiritual conviction of presence. This moment is as far removed as possible from the narrator's disorientation in 'My Father' caused by missing streets in the map of Manchester and misdirected locations.

Adcock's personal quest for ancestral connection embraces multiple perspectives and is capable of plural interpretations: the belief in a transcendent reality is only one possible approach; for the twenty-four poems are interconnected in ways that show how ancestor worship leads the personality to refract and splinter into multiple new points of self-discovery. Reverential worship in 'Beanfield' is juxtaposed with the 'scientific' perspective of 'Ancestor to Devotee'. The ancestor's sceptical questions of her devoted researcher reinscribe the very points under scrutiny:

> What are you loving me with? I'm dead.
> What gland of tenderness throbs in you,
> yearning back through the silt of ages
> to a face and a voice you never knew?

(Poems, 247)

Language itself comes under the microscope through an Enlightenment discourse with its reductive approach to memory and affection and its barren insistence that those relics which the grave conceals are all that remain, creating a tension with Adcock's newly found spiritual energy:

> What's left of me, if you gathered it up,
> is a faggot of bones, some ink-scrawled paper,
> flown-away cells of skin and hair...
> you could set the lot on fire with a taper.

(Poems, 248)

Adcock moves beyond mortality to touch on Puritan eschatology in the final poem, 'Peter Wentworth in Heaven' (*Poems*, 255), about an ancestor famous for having been imprisoned in the Tower by Elizabeth I for demanding increased freedom of speech for Parliament; yet this position as well is comically leavened by Wentworth's complacent dependence on the written word (in ways which refocus and comment on her own endeavour). He and his wife, Elizabeth Walsingham, 'walk together in the orchards of Heaven', their safe conduct guaranteed by the books he has written: 'My *Pithie Exhortation* still exists –/ go and read it in your British Library' and later, 'Read my *Exhortation* and my *Discourse*; / so you may understand me when we come to meet.' Like Thackeray at the end of *Vanity Fair* Adcock's most complete act of deconstruction is to deliberately collapse her creation, so acknowledging the exhaustion of her endeavour – trying to create life from the world beyond the grave. 'Traitors' concludes: 'I see them bundled into a box,/ dismembered toys, still faintly squeaking,/ one with royal blood on his paws.' (*Poems*, 253)

These twenty-four poems are evidence of Adcock's ceaseless search to mark out new territory connected with her family history. The restlessness that characterizes her diasporic identity, strongly apparent in the exploration of space and time in *Time-Zones*, enables her to move adroitly between different generations, genders and family relations and to develop the art of fictive imagining by creating new presences from spaces where before were only words or relics. Working with the most unlikely and insignificant remains – as the lines in 'Ancestor to Devotee' suggest – Adcock's act of bringing the dead back to life is one of devotion which also pays homage to the origins of her art.

8

Conclusion

The preoccupations with identity and location in Adcock's work and the related emphasis on home and belonging are major ones which define important directions in the development of her talents. Her interrogation of these issues, which has involved negotiations of selfhood through the vectors of time as well as place, offers new contexts for understanding the irony, deflation and mock heroics of her work, her preference for a reticent mode, her strong sense of voice from the outset: all require an appreciation of division, and Adcock's acknowledgement of distance and difference through her double displacement in diaspora has led to a growth of her ironic vision. Likewise her registering of the odd, bizarre and the curious as ways of unsettling and redefining the ordinary has undergone transformations that are identifiable with the opening up of new spaces and creation of new moments of origin. In such ways her multiple journeys, plural subjectivities and multi-locational attachments, constitutive of a mode of existence developed over forty years, have mobilized in her verse a searching exploration of various locations, historical moments and encounters.

Issues of identity and location define Adcock's strengths and limitations as a poet: she has always been associated with intimacy and the domestic sphere and this has sometimes led to a perceived slightness of subject matter or archness of voice. Yet her early poems which used conversational address to her children were the foundation of her reputation. Avoiding the grand statement, the totalizing abstraction and the public persona associated with major themes, she has made a virtue of modesty and economy; yet her achievement reveals that the whole is indeed larger than the parts. Her recent preoccupation with discovering and recreating her ancestors, at first an unlikely departure for someone who had been such a decisive presence in the groundswell of women's poetry in Britain in the 1980s, represents another stage in the psychological process of identity formation that Adcock is obsessively engaged with. Her predilection for the motif of retrogression which appears both comically and surrealistically in poems like 'Regression' and 'Last Song' becomes a metaphor for the act of rerouting her life back into the distant past, suggesting that for her this coincides with a return to a simpler state of being, ultimately offering a counter to nostalgia. Genealogical research has opened up a new dimension in her own autobiographical path enabling her to return to her earliest memories and to recapture the innocent space of childhood in ways reminiscent of her early poems to her children.

Among the new poems in *Poems, 1960-2000* are some short, five line poems. They include observations of birds and creatures in Kensington Gardens where Adcock held a poetry placement in 1999, reflections on events that occurred then and 'my love affair with the natural world' (*Poems*, 279). The final poem which opens: 'Goodbye, summer. Poetry goes to bed....' and concludes: 'What wanted to be said is said' (*Poems*, 279), seems to mark the end of a stage in her poetic exploration.[1] But these sentiments are preliminaries to new poetry where Adcock returns to memories of her childhood. The subterranean work of unearthing her ancestors has provided a vital distance from her more negotiated adult desires, a move away from the artifice of rhetoric and an inquiry into the child's consciousness. The early stirrings of creativity recorded in 'Kuaotunu' promise a universe: her recall confirms that memory can confer the prospect of completion.

> ...I'm drawing a face.
> Inside my head I can see it clearly,
>
> but my fingers won't do what I tell them.
> It turns out to be a round patch
> of scribble. It looks more like the world.[2]

Recent poems like this one, 'Linseed', and the sequence, 'My English Childhood', show Adcock embarking on another journey of self-discovery, one which brings her once more full circle.

Notes

CHAPTER 1. INTRODUCTION: A DOUBLE DISPLACEMENT

1. See, e.g., Vernon Scannell, *Critical Quarterly* 29.3 (1987), 106, agreeing with Gavin Ewart: 'The most talented woman poet now writing in Britain'.
2. 'Fleur Adcock talking to Robin Marsack', *Verse* 10.2 (Summer, 1993), 17.
3. 'Fleur Adcock', *Corgi Modern Poets in Focus* 5, ed. Dannie Abse (Corgi: London, 1973), 109.
4. Jane Evans Braziel and Anita Mannur, 'Nation, Migration, Globalization: Points of Contention in Diaspora Studies'. Introduction to *Theorizing Diaspora: A Reader*, ed. Jane Evans Braziel and Anita Mannur (Oxford: Blackwell, 2003), 3, 4–5.
5. Vijay Mishra, 'The diasporic imaginary: theorizing the Indian diaspora', *Textual Practice* 10:3 (1996), 423.
6. Avtah Brah, *Cartographies of Diaspora: Contesting Identities* (London and New York: Routledge, 1996), 16, 180, 193.
7. Roger Bromley, *Narratives for a New Belonging: Diasporic Cultural Fictions* (Edinburgh: Edinburgh University Press, 2000), 5.
8. 'Fleur Adcock', in *The Bloodaxe Book of Contemporary Women Poets: Eleven British Writers*, ed. Jeni Couzyn (Newcastle: Bloodaxe, 1985), 202.
9. This argument is made by Ian Gregson, ' "Your Voice Speaking in My Poems": Polyphony in Fleur Adcock', *Contemporary Poetry and Postmodernism: Dialogue and Estrangement* (London: Macmillan, 1996), 84-96.
10. 'Cultural Identity and Diaspora', *Identity: Community, Culture and Difference*, ed. Jonathan Rutherford (London: Lawrence and Wishart, 1990), 226.
11. See Ella Shohat and Robert Stam, *Unthinking Eurocentrism: Multiculturalism and the Media* (London and New York: Routledge, 1994), 41-46.

12. Andrew Motion, review of *Selected Poems*, *TLS*, 2 September 1983, 922.

13. Homi Bhabha, *The Location of Culture* (London and New York: Routledge, 1994), 5.

14. Andrew Gurr, *Writers in Exile: The Identity of Home in Modern Literature* (Sussex: Harvester Wheatsheaf, 1981), 15–16, 23–24.

15. See Julian Stannard, *Fleur Adcock in Context: From Movement to Martians* (Lampeter: Edwin Mellen Press, 1997).

16. Carmen Zamorana Llena, 'The Location of Identity in the Interstitial Spaces: The Poetry of Fleur Adcock in a Multicultural Britain', *Journal of New Zealand Literature* 18/19 (2000/01), 161–172.

CHAPTER 2. EARLY INFLUENCES: TWO HEMISPHERES AND THE DIVIDED SELF

1. Alan Lawson, 'Postcolonial Theory and the "Settler" Subject', *Essays on Canadian Writing* 56, ed. Diana Brydon (1995): 29.

2. Sally Vincent, 'Final Touch', *Guardian Weekend*, 29 July 2000, 34.

3. Pakeha, meaning stranger or 'foreigner', is commonly used in New Zealand to define the European.

4. See Joy MacKenzie, '"My way is to be with you": Meg and Alistair Te Ariki Campbell', *Between the Lives: Partners in Art*, ed. Deborah Shepherd (Auckland: Auckland University Press, 2005), 203–04.

5. Julian Stannard, 'Interview with Fleur Adcock', *Thumbscrew* 17 (Winter, 2000/1), 6-7.

6. 'Kuaotunu', *Journal of Postcolonial Writing* 41.1 (May, 2005), 110.

7. Stannard, 'Interview with Fleur Adcock', 8.

8. Marilyn Duckworth, 'Cherries on a Plate', in *Cherries on a Plate: New Zealand Writers Talk about their Sisters*, ed. Marilyn Duckworth (Auckland: Random House, 1996), 182. This verse forms the epigraph as well as the title of Marilyn Duckworth's piece on her sister.

9. Vijay Mishra, 'The Diasporic Imaginary: Theorising the Indian Diaspora', *Textual Practice* 10:3 (1996), 423–25.

10. Eva Hoffman, *Lost in Translation: A Life in a New Language* (New York: Penguin, 1990).

11. 'Fleur Adcock', *Talking about Ourselves: Twelve New Zealand Poets in Conversation with Harry Ricketts* (Wellington: Mallinson Rendell, 1986), 130.

12. Bill Ruddick, 'A Clear Channel Flowing: The Poetry of Fleur Adcock', *Critical Quarterly* 26:4 (1984), 61.

13. Peter Childs links Plath and Adcock in representing a post-World

War II disillusionment with marriage; *The Twentieth Century in Poetry: A Critical Survey* (London and New York: Routledge, 1999), 170–72.

14. Emma Neale reads this poem in terms of Adcock's concern with the relationship between 'self and topos'. The focus on the elements and generalized locales of 'city, sea and field', 'plain and mountain', anticipate her antagonistic encounter with New Zealand landscape and subsequent attachments to other landscapes and places; '"Why Can't She Stay Home?" Expatriation and Back Migration in the Work of Katherine Mansfield, Robin Hyde and Fleur Adcock.' PhD. thesis, University College, London, 1999, 275.

15. Childs, *The Twentieth Century in Poetry*, 139.

16. Adcock writes that in order 'to avoid public scrutiny of my character, I used the personal "he" throughout. ... The result was that people assumed the poem to be about my husband'. 'Fleur Adcock' in *Poetry Dimension* 2, ed. Dannie Abse (London: Robson Books, 1974), 232; TWIH, 154–55.

17. 'Beauty Abroad', 'Knife-play' and 'Comment' were excluded from *Tigers*, but restored to the canon in *Selected Poems* (1983).

18. "Why Can't She Stay Home?", 275–77.

19. See early appreciations of this poem by James Bertram, *Landfall* 72. Vol. 18.4 (1964), 371–2; Vincent O'Sullivan, transcript of review for New Zealand Broadcasting Corporation, 12 June 1964, 2.

20. Eluned Summers-Bremner, 'Reading, Walking, Mourning: W.G. Sebald's Peripatetic Fictions', *Journal of Narrative Theory* 34:3 (2004), 309.

21. See Cathy Caruth, Introduction to *Trauma: Explorations in Memory*, ed. Cathy Caruth (Baltimore and London: Johns Hopkins University Press, 1995), 3–12.

22. The inexpressibility topos or *occupatio*, often a sequence of negatives, is frequently used in classical and medieval poetry; the poet emphasizes something while pointedly seeming to pass over it. *A Handlist of Rhetorical Terms*, ed. Richard A. Lanham, 2nd ed. (Berkeley and London: University of California Press, 1991), 104.

23. Julian Stannard, *Fleur Adcock in Context: From Movement to Martians* (Lampeter: Edwin Mellen Press, 1997), 11, compares Adcock to Larkin's evocation of the existential in proclaiming eventlessness: Larkin wrote in 'I Remember, I Remember', 'Nothing, like something, happens anywhere'; Margaret Byers in 'Cautious Vision: Recent British Poetry by Women', in *British Poetry since 1960: A Critical Survey*, ed. Michael Schmidt and Grevel Lindop (Oxford: Carcanet, 1972), 76, notes the speaker's 'almost impotent exertion of will'; the poem's form is intensified to cope with 'a painful experience ... the speaker escapes from form in form'. Neale claims

convincingly that the poem negotiates between two ways of seeing by viewing this world in terms of another. Opposites correlate: 'Stone lions ... gleam like wet seals'; 'stiff' is oxymoronically collocated with 'dripping' in 'the green birds / are stiff with dripping pride'. However I disagree that the persona is awaiting 'a storm, literally and figuratively' and that the poem 'dramatises the nature of suspense'. ("Why Can't She Stay Home?", 282).

CHAPTER 3. HOME, IDENTITY AND BELONGING: ENGLAND 1963–1974

1. This chapter is an expanded version of Janet Wilson, 'Fleur Adcock: ambivalent expatriate, 1964–1974', *Journal of New Zealand Literature* 21 (2003): 54–72.
2. 'Fleur Adcock', *Contemporary Authors Autobiography Series*, ed. Shelley Andrews, 30 vols (Detroit, MI: Gale Research 1984–), 23 (1996) 11–12.
3. Stannard, *Fleur Adcock in Context*; Martin Booth, *British Poetry 1964-1984: Driving through the Barricades* (London: Routledge and Kegan Paul, 1985), 134.
4. *A Group Anthology*, ed. Edward Lucie-Smith (London: Oxford University Press, 1963); *British Poetry since 1945*, ed. E. Lucie-Smith (Harmondsworth: Penguin, 1970); Alan Brownjohn's review of *Poems 1960–2000*, *The Sunday Times*, 16 July, 2000.
5. Ruddick, 'A Clear Channel Flowing', 64.
6. Rod Edmond, '"In Search of the Lost Tribe": Janet Frame's England', *Other Britain, Other British*, ed. Robert A. Lee (London: Pluto Press, 1995), 161-74; Revathi Krishnaswamy, 'Mythologies of Migrancy', *ARIEL* 26:1 (1995), 125–46.
7. Neale, "Why Can't She Stay Home?", 10–12; *An Analysis and Biographical Dictionary of Literary Exile in the Twentieth Century*, ed. Martin Tucker (New York: Greenwood Press, 1991), 15–16.
8. Brah, *Cartographies of Diaspora*, 180, 193.
9. 'Fleur Adcock', *Contemporary Authors*, 1.
10. Ibid., 12.
11. Adcock has commented that the criteria were mainly artistic; the volume's arrangement was partly due to the editorial advice of George MacBeth.
12. Margaret Byers, 'Cautious Vision: Recent British Poetry by Women', *British Poetry Since 1960: A Critical Survey*, ed. Michael Schmidt and Grevel Lindop (Manchester: Carcanet Press, 1972), 76, notes the poem is 'latently autobiographical'; Emma Neale points out that

'Hamilton' is a name of Adcock's maternal ancestors in 'Please Identify Yourself' ("Why Can't She Stay Home?", 304).

13. In *Tigers* 'The Lover' follows 'For Andrew'. It is not included in the 1983 *Selected Poems*.

14. 'Fleur Adcock', *Corgi Modern Poets in Focus* 5, ed. Dannie Abse (London: Corgi, 1973), 105–06.

15. 'DissemiNation: time, narrative, and the margins of the modern nation', *Nation and Narration*, ed. Homi Bhabha (London and New York: Routledge, 1990), 307.

16. Jonathan Rutherford, 'The Third Space: Interview with Homi Bhabha', *Identity, Community, Culture, Difference*, ed. Jonathan Rutherford (London: Lawrence and Wishart, 1990), 210.

17. *The Location of Culture* (London and New York: Routledge, 1994), 2.

18. Adcock writes that the setting was probably 'Aden or the Arabian peninsula; Aden was much in the news in 1966 or 1967 when I wrote the poem', or 'possibly Greece which I had recently visited.... But I left the place deliberately vague, to add to the sense of menace.' Letter to pupils at Bandon Grammar School, Cork, Ireland (1980).

19. C.K. Stead, 'Fleur Adcock: A Cool Intelligence', *In the Glass Case: Essays on New Zealand Literature* (Auckland: Auckland University Press, 1979), 237.

20. 'Fleur Adcock', *The Bloodaxe Book of Contemporary Women Poets: Eleven British Writers*, ed. Jeni Couzyn (Newcastle: Bloodaxe, 1985), 200.

21. Kevin Cunningham reviewing *Tigers*, *Landfall* 84. Vol. 21:4 (1967), 391–95; his conclusion 'Miss Adcock just doesn't seem to have anything to say' inspired a poem from Charles Brasch in *Landfall* 85. Vol. 22:1 (1968), 113. Michael Hulse, reviewing *Selected Poems*, *Quadrant* 28:2 (January-February 1984), 52–53, also says 'Adcock has made no attempt to make anything of her material'.

22. Michael Hofmann reviewing *The Incident Book*, TLS, 13 February 1987: 35, finds in the anecdotal 'Schools' section 'an uncomfortable patness about many of the endings'.

23. Vona Grodarke, *PN Review* 124 (November-December 1998), 65–66.

24. *Thumbscrew* 10 (Spring, 1998), 125.

25. 'Old and New Identities, Old and New Ethnicities', *Culture, Globalization and the World-System*, ed. Anthony D. King (London: Macmillan, 1991), 47.

26. Ruddick, 'A Clear Channel Flowing,' 62.

27. She writes: 'it was a kind of threnody for several of my great aunts and uncles who had died in New Zealand while I was on the other side of the world'. TWIH, 150.

28. 'The Local and the Global: Globalization and Ethnicity', *Culture, Globalization and the World-System*, 21.

CHAPTER 4.   TO AND FRO: LIVING IN DIASPORA

1. 'C.K. Stead and Fleur Adcock: A Conversation', *Landfall* 181. Vol. 46:1 (1992): 42; 'Fleur Adcock', *The Bloodaxe Book of Contemporary Women Poets*, 202; Stannard, 'Interview with Fleur Adcock', 15.
2. Adcock excluded her own verse and that of Kevin Ireland because expatriation: 'leads to a subtle but distinct alteration in one's consciousness and attitudes: without ceasing to be a New Zealander one develops a view of the world whose focus is elsewhere ... poetry written from such an outlook cannot rightly be called New Zealand poetry'. Introduction to *The Oxford Book of Contemporary New Zealand Poetry* (Auckland: OUP, 1982), viii. See Lauris Edmond's interview with Fleur Adcock, *Landfall* 143. Vol. 36:3 (1982): 320–6.
3. Roger Bromley, *Narratives for a New Belonging*, 3.
4. 'Fleur Adcock', in *The Oxford Companion to New Zealand Literature*, ed. Roger Robinson and Nelson Wattie (Oxford: OUP, 1998), 4.
5. R. Rhadhakrishnan, 'Ethnicity in an Age of Diaspora', *Theorizing Diaspora*, 123.
6. Christine Sheehy, 'The Resurrected Muse', *New Zealand Listener*, 1 July 2006, 37.
7. Adcock says it was 'very traumatic engaging with parts of my past I had tried to forget about'. Stannard, 'Interview with Fleur Adcock', 10.
8. Braziel and Mannur, 'Nation, Migration, Globalization', *Theorizing Diaspora*, 5.
9. By contrast, her schools in Surrey, still flourishing when she returns, symbolize continuity between the present and the past.
10. See TWIH, 156–7. Adcock also uses 'you' impersonally, as a 'raconteur's pronoun', and a substitute for 'one'.
11. MacD. P. Jackson and Elizabeth Caffin, 'Poetry' in *The Oxford History of New Zealand Literature*, ed. Terry Sturm (Oxford: OUP, 1991), 409.
12. Pamela Tomlinson, *Islands* 29 (June 1980), 173–5, says the relationship truly expressed becomes itself a 'poem', a union of contrasts.
13. 'Fleur Adcock', *Corgi Modern Poets in Focus*, 108.
14. 'The description of the appearance of a person; real or imaginary'. *A Handlist of Rhetorical Terms*, 123.
15. Linda Hardy, 'The Ghost of Katherine Mansfield', *Landfall* 172. Vol. 43:4 (1989): 421–2.
16. 'Surridge' is the local mispronunciation of 'sewerage'. It is also the name of Stuart Surridge, Surrey's greatest cricket captain of the 1950s, and so this rhyme can be read as mock heroic. I am grateful to J.R. Pole for this information.

CHAPTER 5.   INTERROGATIONS: GENDER ISSUES

1. Carol Ann Duffy, Review of *Time-Zones*. *Guardian*, 14 November, 1991.
2. R. Radhakrishnan, 'Nationalism, Gender and Identity', in *Postcolonial Discourses: An Anthology*, ed. Gregory Castle (Oxford: Blackwell, 2001), 193, argues that the place of women is a kind of *dis*placement.
3. 'Fleur Adcock', *The Bloodaxe Book of Contemporary Women Poets*, 202.
4. 'Fleur Adcock', *Poets Talking*, 34–5.
5. In an interview with Lauris Edmond she stresses that feminism seems the province of the privileged, 'not those who really need to be liberated'. *Landfall* 143. Vol. 36.3 (1982), 324.
6. Introduction to *The Faber Book of Twentieth Century Women's Poetry*, ed. Fleur Adcock (London; Faber, 1987), 1–2; 'Fleur Adcock', *Poets Talking*, 34.
7. Stannard, 'Interview with Fleur Adcock', 14.
8. Andrew Motion, review of *Selected Poems*, TLS, 2 September 1983, 922.
9. Ian Gregson, ' "Your Voice Speaking in My Poems" ', 85, 88.
10. Motion, review of *Selected Poems*, 922.
11. 'Fleur Adcock', *Poets Talking*, 32.
12. 'In my early poems were few women, apart from fabulised and fictionalised versions of myself ... .I had to play most of the female roles myself.' *Bloodaxe Book of Contemporary Women Poets*, 202.
13. 'Fleur Adcock', *Poets Talking*, 33–4.
14. Emma Neale, 'Why Can't She Stay Home?', 301, 312-13, comments that Adcock's irony is often evasive and defensive.
15. 'Fleur Adcock', *Corgi Modern Poets in Focus*, 105.
16. See Ian Gregson's interpretation of the 'dialogue of gender' and the use of free indirect discourse in this poem; ' "Your Voice Speaking in my Poems" ', 96.
17. Trevor James, review of *The Inner Harbour*, *Landfall* 136. Vol. 32:4 (1980), 194–8.
18. Gregson, ' "Your Voice Speaking in my Poems" ', 92–3, argues that the "unstable" compound of voices in 'Tokens' shows Adcock refusing to let gender distinctions settle or synthesize.
19. See Chapter 4, p. 54.
20. Alan Robinson, *Instabilities in Contemporary British Poetry* (London: Macmillan, 1988), 189, quoted by Peter Childs in *The Twentieth Century in Poetry*, 170–2.
21. Raman Selden, *Practising Theory and Reading Literature: An Introduction* (Hemel Hempstead: Harvester Wheatsheaf, 1989), 149–52.

Adcock refutes Selden's claim that the opening alludes to George Herbert's 'Vanite': the poem's genesis was its title which came to her 'in a half-dreaming state' and suggested to her the Ex-Queen Soraya (divorced because she was infertile); i.e. from a non-western society where women were expected to please men. Stannard, *Fleur Adcock in Context*, 67–8, finds that the interchange of sexual and astronomical imagery makes the poem 'truly cosmic'. Pamela Tomlinson, *Islands* 29 (June 1980), 173–5, claims that the 'poem's confident muscularity seems to match its subject'; Edna Longley, *TLS*, 18 January 1980, 64, claims the poem 'possesses the imaginative and female powers it asserts'; Andrew Motion, *TLS* 2 September 1983, says the 'narrative gains marvellous intensity by refusing to give more than the most tantalizingly reticent articulation of its theme'.

22. Luce Irigarary, *Speculum of the other Woman*, tr. Gillian C. Gill (Ithaca: Cornell University Press, 1985), 229.
23. See Kay Schaffer, 'Colonizing Gender in Colonial Australia: The Eliza Fraser Story', *Writing Women and Space: Colonial and Postcolonial Geographies*, ed. Alison Blunt and Gillian Rose (London and New York: Guilford Press, 1994), 106.
24. Claude Rawson, review of *Selected Poems. Poetry Review*, 73:3 (1983), 61.

CHAPTER 6.   CREATURES, JOURNEYS, ECO-POLITICS

1. Carmen Zamorana Llena, 'Location of Identity', 169, says of the hyphen: '... time and zones, histories and geographies, come closer together to form new hybrid identities'.
2. See *The Oxford Book of Creatures*, ed. Fleur Adcock and Jacqueline Simms (Oxford: OUP, 1995).
3. Review of *Time-Zones, London Review of Books*, 9 January 1992, 22–3; Carol Ann Duffy, reviewing *Time-Zones, Guardian*, 14 November 1991, says 'she picks at [nostalgia] like a scab'.
4. Clair Wills, review of *Time-Zones, TLS*, 30 August 1991.
5. Brah, *Cartographies of Diaspora*, 181, 209.

CHAPTER 7.   SEEKING THE ANCESTORS

1. I am grateful to Adcock for showing me two unpublished prose accounts of her father's life and her childhood: 'Sam, Eva and Cyril' and 'England and After'.
2. Brah, *Cartographies of Diaspora*, 197.

3. Emma Neale, "Why Can't She Stay Home?", 271.
4. Homi K. Bhabha, Keynote lecture 'Minority Culture and Creative Anxiety,' *Re-Inventing Britain* Conference (British Council, 1997); 16 March 2007, <www.counterpoint-online.org>. That 'translation' is part of Adcock's attempt in verse, is noted by John Greening, review of *Poems 1960–2000*, *TLS*, 21 July 2000, 25.
5. Neale, 'Why Can't She Stay Home?', 301.
6. 'Fleur Adcock', *Contemporary Authors*, 2.
7. See Stannard, 'Interview with Fleur Adcock', 8, on this poem.
8. Stannard, *Fleur Adcock in Context*, 35–6.
9. 'Fleur Adcock', *Poets Talking*, 23: 'I like grammar and punctuation and the general elements of order in discourse ... it's all a way of just putting a straitjacket around the mad wailing hysterical self inside'. A similar formal breakdown due to emotional crisis appears in the ellipses of 'Having No Mind for the Same Poem'.

CHAPTER 8.   CONCLUSION

1. Sheehy, 'The Resurrected Muse', 36.
2. *Journal of Postcolonial Writing* 41.1 (May, 2005): 110.

Select Bibliography

WORKS BY FLEUR ADCOCK

(a) Poetry
The Eye of the Hurricane (Wellington and Auckland: A.H. and A.W. Reed, 1964).
Tigers (London: OUP, 1967).
High Tide in the Garden (London: OUP, 1971).
The Scenic Route (London: OUP, 1974).
The Inner Harbour (London and New York: OUP, 1979).
Below Loughrigg (Newcastle: Bloodaxe, 1979).
Selected Poems (Oxford: OUP, 1983).
Hotspur: A Ballad for Music, music by Gillian Whitehead, monoprints by Gretchen Albrecht (Newcastle: Bloodaxe Books, 1986).
The Incident Book (Oxford: OUP, 1986).
Meeting the Comet (Newcastle: Bloodaxe Books, 1988).
Time-Zones (Oxford: OUP, 1991).
Looking Back (Oxford: OUP, 1997).
Poems 1960-2000 (Newcastle: Bloodaxe Books, 2000).
'The Ex-Poet', *Guardian Weekend,* July 29 2000.
'Linseed', *TLS,* 6 March 2004.
'An Observation', *TLS,* 19 March 2004.
'My English Childhood', *PN Review* 159. Vol. 31.1 (September-October, 2004).
'Kuaotunu', *Journal of Postcolonial Writing* 41.1 (May, 2005), 110.

(b) Editions by Fleur Adcock
(With Anthony Thwaite) *New Poetry* 4 (London: Hutchinson, 1978).
The Oxford Book of Contemporary New Zealand Poetry (Auckland: OUP, 1982).
The Faber Book of Twentieth Century Women's Poetry (London: Faber, 1987).
(With Jacqueline Simms) *The Oxford Book of Creatures* (Oxford: OUP,

1995).

(c) Edition and Translation by Fleur Adcock

Hugh Primas and the Archpoet, Cambridge Medieval Classics 2 (Cambridge: Cambridge University Press, 1994).

(d) Translations by Fleur Adcock

The Virgin and the Nightingale: Medieval Latin Lyrics (Newcastle: Bloodaxe Books, 1983).
Grete Tartler, *Orient Express* (Oxford: OUP, 1989).
Daniela Crasnaru, *Letters from Darkness* (Oxford: OUP, 1991).

(e) Autobiographical Writings by Fleur Adcock

'Women as Poets: Fleur Adcock' in *Poetry Dimension* 2, ed. Dannie Abse (London: Robson Books, 1974), 229–34.
'Beginnings', *Islands* 26 (1979), 347–56.
'Rural Blitz: Fleur Adcock's English Childhood', *Poetry Review* 74:2 (June, 1984): 5–12.
'Fleur Adcock', in Jeni Couzyn, ed. *The Bloodaxe Book of Contemporary Women Poets: Eleven British Writers* (Newcastle: Bloodaxe, 1985), 200–02.
'A Lifetime of Writing', *Beyond Expectations, Fourteen New Zealand Women Write about their Lives*, ed. Margaret Clark (Wellington: Allen & Unwin/Port Nicholson Press, 1986), 99–112.
'The Way it Happens', *The Poet's Voice and Craft*, ed. C.B. McCully (Manchester: Carcanet Press, 1994), 147–65.
'Fleur Adcock', *Contemporary Authors Autobiography Series*, ed. Shelley Andrews, 30 vols (Detroit, MI: Gale Research 1984-), 23 (1996), 1–17.
'Bluebell Seasons', *Cherries on a Plate: New Zealand Writers Talk about their Sisters*, ed. Marilyn Duckworth (Auckland: Random House, 1996), 220–45.
'Not Quite a Statement', *Strong Words: Modern Poets on Modern Poetry*, ed. W.N. Herbert and Matthew Hollis (Tarset: Bloodaxe, 2000), 198–200.

INTERVIEWS, BIOGRAPHIES, LETTERS

Duckworth, Marilyn, 'Cherries on a Plate', in *Cherries on a Plate: Writers Talk about their Sisters*, ed. Marilyn Duckworth (Auckland: Random House, 1996), 182–215.
Edmond, Lauris, 'Interview with Fleur Adcock', *Landfall* 143. Vol. 36.3

(1982), 320–6.

Marsack, Robyn, 'Fleur Adcock talking to Robyn Marsack', *Verse* 10:2 (Summer, 1993), 9–18.

Ricketts, Harry, 'Fleur Adcock', *Talking about Ourselves: Twelve New Zealand Poets in Conversation with Harry Ricketts* (Wellington: Mallinson Rendel, 1986), 124–33.

Sheehy, Christine, 'The Resurrected Muse', *New Zealand Listener*, 1 July 2006, 36–7.

Stannard, Julian, 'Interview with Fleur Adcock', *Thumbscrew* 17 (Winter, 2000/1), 5–15.

Stead, C.K., 'C.K. Stead and Fleur Adcock: A Conversation', *Landfall* 181. Vol. 46.1 (March 1992), 42–64.

Wilmer, Clive, 'Fleur Adcock', in *Poets Talking: Poet of the Month Interviews from BBC Radio 3* (Manchester: Carcanet Press, 1994), 28–35.

CRITICAL STUDIES AND REVIEWS

Abse, Dannie, 'Fleur Adcock', in *Corgi Modern Poet in Focus* 5 (Corgi: London, 1973), 101–09. Introductory overview of early work; includes comment by Adcock on her work.

Allnutt, Gillian, 'Genealogies'. Review of *Looking Back, Poetry Review* 88.1 (Spring 1998), 95–6. Appreciates Adcock's humour and valuing of 'a kind of love' in poems on her ancestors.

Bertram, James, Review of *The Eye of the Hurricane*, *Landfall* 72. Vol. 18.4 (1964), 369–72. Praises Adcock's taste in classical irony and rates the conversation poems with children as the most successful.

Brownjohn, Alan, Review of *The Inner Harbour*, *Encounter* 53 (1979), 49.
———— 'A Fertile Flowering', Review of *Poems 1960–2000. The Sunday Times*, 16 July 2000. Poems written to those closest to her are the most impressive for their emotional commitment.

Byers, Margaret, 'Cautious Vision: Recent British Poetry by Women', in *British Poetry Since 1960: A Critical Survey*, ed. Michael Schmidt and Grevel Lindop (Manchester: Carcanet Press, 1972), 75–7. Astute study of *Tigers*, comparing Adcock's handling of fluctuation between areas of consciousness to Elizabeth Bishop and Iris Murdoch.

Childs, Peter, *The Twentieth Century in Poetry: A Critical Survey* (London: Routledge, 1999). Argues that gender dominates the divisions of identity in Adcock's work; she shares with Sylvia Plath anxieties about motherhood, marriage and sexuality.

Cunningham, Kevin, Review of *Tigers*, *Landfall* 84. Vol. 21:1 (1967): 391–5. Criticizes her detachment. His complaint 'that Miss Adcock just doesn't seem to have anything to say', sparked a controversy in New Zealand with both Charles Brasch, editor of *Landfall*, and James K.

Baxter coming to her defence.

Dowson, Jane, 'Anthologies of Women's Poetry', in *British Poetry from the 1950s to the 1990s: Politics and Art*, ed. Gary Day and Brian Docherty (London: Macmillan, 1997), 237–51. Useful study of Adcock's place in the 'Renaissance' of women's poetry in the 1980s which comments on her selection of the Faber anthology.

Duffy, Carol Ann, 'Haunted by the Flower', review of *Time-Zones*, *Guardian*, 14 November 1991.

Greening, John, 'Plainly Daring', review of *Poems 1960-2000*, *TLS*, 21 July 2000, 25. Praises the freshness of her 'New Plain Style' and the witty surprises in her work.

Gregson, Ian, ' "Your Voice Speaking in my Poems": Polyphony in Fleur Adcock', *Contemporary Poetry and Postmodernism: Dialogue and Estrangement* (London: Macmillan, 1996), 84–96. Sees Adcock's 'cultural displacement' as a synechdoche for psychological disorientation. Excellent readings of poems focussing on her 'dialogue of genders'.

Grodarke, Vona, 'Other-Worldly Poetry', review of *Looking Back*, *PN Review* 124 (November–December 1998), 65–6. Commends Adcock's tact in the risky process of recreating history; finds poems in the second half, more lightweight by comparison.

Hardy, Linda, 'The Ghost of Katherine Mansfield', *Landfall* 172. Vol. 43.4 (December 1989), 416–32. Argues that KM is a phantasmic and sometimes troubling sign of displacement. Claims that 'Villa Isola Bella' shows no trace of an influence of Mansfield on Adcock.

Hofman, Michael, 'Malice in Thatcherland', review of *The Incident Book*, *TLS*, 13 February 1987, 67. Writes that the best poems are about England; but there is a 'lack of real substance'.

Hulse, Michael, 'Fleur Adcock: A Poet with Bite', review of *Selected Poems*, *Quadrant* 28: 1–2 (January-February 1984): 52–3. Considers it an uneven work which does not always 'make' anything of her material; but the personal poems are tender and unsentimental.

James, Trevor, 'Fleur Adcock and Alan Loney', *Landfall* 136. Vol. 32.4 (1980), 194–98. Review of *The Inner Harbour*. Feels that Adcock's detachment is often unsatisfactory as a pose; there are signs of estrangement in sexual relationships; yet a movement into the self with personal, imaginative freedom.

Llena, Carmen Zamorana, 'The Location of Identity in the Interstitial Spaces: The Poetry of Fleur Adcock in a Multicultural Britain', *Journal of New Zealand Literature* 18/19 (2000/1), 161–72. Explains that Adcock is a British-New Zealand hybrid, whose physical location in England required a 'psychological return' to New Zealand. Adcock and her New Zealand-British ethnicity can be seen as part of alternative, multi-cultural Britain.

123

Longley, Edna, 'The British', *Times Literary Supplement*, 18 January 1980, 64.

Lucas, John, 'Art for Heart's Sake', *New Statesman*, 28 November 1986, 31.

Motion, Andrew, review of *Selected Poems*, *TLS*, 2 September 1983, 922.

Neale, Emma, 'Fleur Adcock', in *The Oxford Companion to New Zealand Literature*, ed. Roger Robinson and Nelson Wattie (Oxford: OUP, 1998).

————— 'Why Can't She Stay Home?' Expatriation and Back Migration in the Work of Katherine Mansfield, Robin Hyde and Fleur Adcock.' PhD. thesis, University College, London, 1999. Significant study of Adcock's troubled relationship to New Zealand in comparison to other New Zealand women writers of exile, Katherine Mansfield, Robin Hyde and Janet Frame, arguing that return to New Zealand in Adcock's case leads to 'reiteration of insoluble debates over identity'.

O'Sullivan, Vincent, transcript of review of *The Eye of the Hurricane* broadcast by the YC stations, The New Zealand Broadcasting Corporation. 12 June 1964.

Pykett, Lyn, 'Women Poets and "Women's Poetry"', *British Poetry from the 1950s to the 1990s: Politics and Art*, ed. Gary Day and Brian Docherty (London: Macmillan, 1997), 253–67. Useful study of Adcock's complex relationship towards feminism.

Rawson, Claude, 'Telling Stories', review of *Selected Poems*, *Poetry Review* 73:3 (1983), 58–61.

Ruddick, Bill, 'A Clear Channel Flowing; The Poetry of Fleur Adcock', *Critical Quarterly* 26: 4 (1984), 61–66. Important review of *Selected Poems* and *The Virgin and the Nightingale*, for its recognition of placelesssness in the New Zealand poems and appraisal of her work as 'lucid, economical and precise in its command of word and metre'.

Rumens, Carol, 'Chatting up the Ancestors', review of *Looking Back*, *Thumbscrew* 10 (Spring 1998), 125–29. Considers this a mixed success due to Adcock's 'idiomatic handicaps' and the emotional 'present-ness' of such an enterprise, combined with her striking ability to evoke sensation and guy her own chattiness.

Scannell, Vernon. 'Recent Poetry', review of *The Incident Book*, *Critical Quarterly* 29.3 (1987), 104–07.

Shapcott, Jo, review of *Looking Back*, *TLS*, October 16 1998, 25. 'Adcock's teasing voice is at her best in the sequence on her ancestors.'

Smith, Stan, 'Imagining the Suburbs', review of *Time-Zones*, *London Review of Books*, 9 January 1992, 22–3.

Stannard, Julian, *Fleur Adcock in Context: From Movement to Martians* (Lampeter: Edwin Mellen Press, 1997). The most extensive study of Adcock to date. Draws on British post-World War II anthologies to identify her as a Group poet who also has affinities with Martian

poets, Craig Raine and Christopher Reid in her 'ludic conscious-
ness'. Limited appraisal of her autobiographical and sociological
contexts.

Stead, C.K. 'Fleur Adcock: A Cool Intelligence', In the Glass Case: Essays
on New Zealand Literature (Auckland: Auckland University Press,
1981), 234–7. His review of High Tide in the Garden distinguishes
between mere accomplishment and 'the conjugations of actual pain
and pleasure' and praises the tension in the New Zealand poems.

Thwaite, Anthony, Poetry Today: A Critical Guide to British Poetry, 1960–95
(London: British Council, 1996), 15. Adcock's 'elegant, colloquial,
astringent, ironical poems' helped establish a public discourse about
gender in Britain in the 1980s; 'did she catch the tone or did she help
to achieve it?'

Tomlinson, Pamela, 'A Widening View', review of The Inner Harbour and
Below Loughrigg, Islands, 29 (June, 1980): 173–5. The Inner Harbour sees
her 'as deeply enmeshed as ever' with New Zealand; Below Loughrigg
has a 'greater ease and security'.

Wills, Clair, 'The Time and the Place', review of Time-Zones, TLS, 30
August, 1991. Believes that the most successful poems are those
whose poetic form realizes the interlocking of time-zones, for
'Adcock is concerned with how the passage between spatial zones
organises our experience of time'.

Wilson, Janet, 'Fleur Adcock: Ambivalent Expatriate, 1964–1974', Journal
of New Zealand Literature, 21 (2003), 54–72.

OTHER WORKS MENTIONED IN THE TEXT

Bhabha, Homi K., Keynote lecture 'Minority Culture and Creative
Anxiety,' Re-Inventing Britain Conference (British Council, 1997) 16
March 2007, <www.counterpoint-online.org>.
———— The Location of Culture (London and New York: Routledge,
1994).
———— 'The Third Space: Interview with Homi Bhabha' in Identity,
Community, Culture, Difference, ed. Jonathan Rutherford (London:
Lawrence and Wishart, 1990), 207–21.
———— 'DissemiNation: time, narrative, and the margins of the
modern nation', in Nation and Narration, ed. Homi Bhabha (London
and New York: Routledge, 1990), 307.
Booth, Martin, British Poetry 1964–1984: Driving through the Barricades
(London: Routledge and Kegan Paul, 1985).
Brah, Avtah, Cartographies of Diaspora: Contesting Identities (London and
New York: Routledge, 1996).
Braziel, Jana Evans and Anita Manur, ed, Theorizing Diaspora: A Reader

(Oxford: Blackwell, 2003).

────── 'Nation, Migration, Globalization: Points of Contention in Diaspora Studies'. Introduction to *Theorizing Diaspora: A Reader,* ed. Jane Evans Braziel and Anita Manur (Oxford: Blackwell, 2003), 1–22.

Bromley, Roger, *Narratives for a New Belonging: Diasporic Cultural Fictions* (Edinburgh: Edinburgh University Press, 2000).

Caruth, Cathy, Introduction to *Trauma: Explorations in Memory,* ed. Cathy Caruth (Baltimore and London: Johns Hopkins University Press, 1995), 3–12.

Childs, Peter, *The Twentieth Century in Poetry: A Critical Survey* (London: Routledge, 1999).

Edmond, Rod, ' "In Search of the Lost Tribe": Janet Frame's England', in *Other Britain, Other British: Contemporary Multicultural Fiction,* ed. A. Robert Lee, (London: Pluto Press, 1995).

Gurr, Andrew, *Writers in Exile: The Identity of Home in Modern Literature* (Sussex: Harvester Wheatsheaf, 1981).

Hall, Stuart, 'Cultural Identity and Diaspora', in *Identity: Community, Culture and Difference,* ed. Jonathan Rutherford (London: Lawrence and Wishart, 1990), 222–37.

────── 'Old and New Identities: Old and New Ethnicities', in *Culture, Globalization and the World-System,* ed. Anthony D. King (London: Macmillan, 1991).

────── 'The Local and the Global: Globalization and Ethnicity', in *Culture, Globalization and the World-System,* ed. Anthony D. King (London: Macmillan, 1991).

Hardy, Linda, 'The Ghost of Katherine Mansfield', *Landfall* 172, Vol. 43:4 (December 1989), 416–32.

Hoffman, Eva, *Lost in Translation: A Life in a New Language* (New York: Penguin, 1990).

Jackson, MacD. P. and Elizabeth Caffin, 'Poetry', in *The Oxford Companion to New Zealand Literature,* ed. Terry Sturm (Oxford: Oxford University Press, 1991), 335–449.

Krishnaswamy, Revathi, 'Mythologies of Migrancy', *ARIEL* 26:1 (1995): 125–46.

Lawson, Alan, 'Postcolonial Theory and the "Settler" Subject', *Essays on Canadian Writing* 56, ed. Diana Brydon (1995), 20–36.

Lanham, Richard A. ed. *A Handlist of Rhetorical Terms,* 2nd ed. (Berkeley and London: University of California Press, 1991), 104.

Lee, Robert A. ed. *Other Britain, Other British: Contemporary Multicultural Fiction* (London: Pluto Press, 1995).

Lucie-Smith, Edward, ed. *British Poetry since 1945* (Harmondsworth: Penguin, 1970).

MacKenzie, Joy. ' "My way is to be with you": Meg and Alistair Te Ariki Campbell', in *Between the Lives: Partners in Art,* ed. Deborah Shepherd

(Auckland: Auckland University Press, 2005), 187–209.

Mills, Sarah, Lynne Pearce, Sue Spaull, Elaine, Millard, *Feminist Readings: Feminists Reading* (Hemel Hempstead: Harvester Wheatsheaf, 1989).

Mishra, Vijay, 'The Diasporic Imaginary: Theorizing the Indian Diaspora', *Textual Practice* 10:3 (1996), 125–46.

Radhakrishnan, R., 'Ethnicity in an Age of Diaspora', in *Theorizing Diaspora: A Reader*, ed. Jane Evans Braziel and Anita Manur (Oxford: Blackwell, 2003), 119–31.

——— 'Nationalism, Gender and Identity', in *Postcolonial Discourses: An Anthology*, ed. Gregory Castle (Oxford: Blackwell, 2001), 191–205.

Schaffer, Kay, 'Colonizing Gender in Colonial Australia: The Eliza Fraser Story', in *Writing Women and Space: Colonial and Postcolonial Geographies*, ed. Alison Blunt and Gillian Rose (London and New York: Guilford Press, 1994), 101–19.

Summers-Bremner, Eluned, 'Reading, Walking, Mourning: W.G. Sebald's Peripatetic Fictions', *Journal of Narrative Theory* 34:3 (2004), 304–34.

Tucker, Martin, ed. *An Analysis and Biographical Dictionary of Literary Exile in the Twentieth Century* (New York: Greenwood Press, 1991).

Appendix

Poems from *The Eye of the Hurricane* which have not been reprinted and which are referred to in the text.

Invocation For Gregory

When the wind's deluding grace
makes the trees and waters wild,
or when the sun pursues its race
over city, sea and field, –
sun, shine gently in the place
where you see my gentle child;
wind grow still before his face:
all the elements, be mild.

Now that I, with voice nor hand,
cannot touch him with my care,
I deputise it to the wind:
let the northward stream of air
flowing over plain and mountain
weave around his chafing fear
unseen its passive cool affection,
while I burn in silence here.

Let the impulses that start,
born to die without their end,
the halted gestures of my heart, –
words, caresses, movements, – blend
and be directed to his mind.
The bird cries outside the nest,
darkness throbs. What I would find
give to my son: be his rest.

The Lover

Always he would inhabit an alien landscape,
someone else's setting; he walked with surly
devotion the moist paths of a bush valley
whose trees had spoken to one he could not keep
as friend; he would learn local names, claim kinship
by an act of will; then let his mind haunt
and cling as hands grasped branches, stones,
eyes learnt by heart another sky's shape.

In late childhood he had lived a year
emotionally wedded to an elm, whose leaves
crumbling in all his pockets evoked rough
and bitter the warm bark; then a small creek
had filled one summer with the breathing air
of willows and brown water; by such loving
he cast off abounding, more exacting dreams,
and baffled others less than he would think.

Later, his enlarging world demanded
mountains, passionate rivers, a harsh bay,
as wider symbols; where no loved face
spread to his hand, he would stroke the wind-grained wood,
learn and cherish a stone's contours, and,
where once the grace of a girl's voice had spoken,
set blind feet on the hare's path to walk
and closet with a rock his loving blood.

The climax never came; he might have cooled
his flesh utterly in the sudden river,
or found long satisfaction in a haven
made solitary by hills; but gradually
the challenging lust ebbed back unfulfilled.
Now, set apart, he lets the city's plan
absorb him calmly; only now and then
stares at the harbour, at the vivid sea.

Summer is Gone

Summer has gone to another country;
the lazy wind awakes from the pole
to herd its clouds. The sky comes lower.
Trees have no more use for their leaves.

Sensitive pores are closed in the stalk
when the leaf is fallen; now the elms

that we saw green from the window together
reveal their structure in barren twigs.

Summer has gone to another country;
the sun that sets on Trinidad
sets for your ship in moors of cloud
banked in a dream's experienced landscape.

Here, trees have no use for their leaves,
branches are numb, the sap sealed in,
the sky constricting, the wind unanchored:
summer is gone to another country.

The Beanstalk

Who eats no beans may grow them:
Pythagorean Jack
swung the stringy ladder
from earth to sky and back.

Lodged in that leafy kitchen
he heard the portent speak
in thundering chords of rhythm –
not, certainly, in Greek.

The astral ceilings echoed,
and, at the tyrant's word,
mysteries were uncovered:
the emblematic bird

teemed with gold; the harp-strings
sang into Jack's ears
(seduction for the simple)
the music of the spheres.

To such a combination
of dazzling sound and sight
what answer? How encompass
that capture and that flight?

Posit a prosperous ending,
with Jack a millionaire:
who could believe it, knowing
that in the upper air

nothing dwells but weather,
that harmony is found
only in mathematics,
and gold beneath the ground?

No: on the fallen beanstalk
the hen, with yellow eye,
clucks a dull derision
of ladders to the sky.

The Witch

The jars of dragon's blood, the dried scarabs
and the small stuffed crocodile proclaim her trade.
Just a hobby she calls it, though – her spells
purely experimental, her drugs home-made.

The early morning scrambles among rocks
for odorous herbs afford, she says, fresh air
and exercise; as for her ancient books,
their cultural worth is the attraction there.

Still, the dark business had a hold on her:
that she admits. And through the years, somehow,
her trade has grown – why not, since it is free?
Her latest client stands before her now,

wincing as the green light strikes his eyes;
he sees thick drops from the alembic fall
into a flask; then, taking it from her hands,
shivers and seems to shrink; but she stands tall.

The Eye of the Hurricane

Ringed about with black fire
we see the lightning crackle in our vineyards;

the burnt and smoking air rises,
dark with wine-fumes, in a dead spiral,

and to our left the sea boils
inward on spastic waves. Only above

the sky is held in a tight bowl
of rigid calm. Here, once, in a different quietness,

careless with fishing-boats and warm
with a milky breeze, we walked the waves' edge,

swam naked in the rollicking sea,
and lay on the sand eating cool grapes

smooth to the sucking tongue, their seeds
gritty as we crushed them with laughing teeth.

There were dragons then, salamanders
trickling among the rocks; and the lemon-tree flowered.

How long is it since we saw
the horizon churning about us in a vortex,

how long since we were trapped in stillness?
Our crops are smouldering now on the grey slopes,

The air thickens with ash. Soon,
as we look towards each other in sick desire

(eyes blank to kinder feelings),
the impatient wind will turn inwards and choke us.

Night-Piece

I *Beginning*

I am afraid of your deep world.
And yet I turn to you, from those
with whom I swung in cadences of sunshine;
those whose flesh was fruit to my mouth, whose skin
smooth as apple-rind and their eyes golden;
who tasted of wine and honey.

Now I move on a different axis.
With you I gaze through the close channel
of a telescope at half-predictable stars;
talking together, we trace their cogent circles,
and making love, we sink down through a dark
well, into sweet water.

II *Before Sleep*

Lying close to your heart-beat, my lips
touching the pulse in our neck, my head on your arm,
I listen to your hidden blood as it slips
with a small furry sound along the warm
veins; and my slowly-flowering dream
of Chinese landscapes, river-banks and flying
splits into sudden shapes – children who scream
by a roadside, blinded men, a woman lying
in a bed filled with blood: the broken ones.
We are so vulnerable. I curl towards
that intricate machine of nerves and bones
with its built-in life: your body. And to your words
I whisper 'Yes' and 'Always', as I lie
waiting for thunder from a stony sky.

III *Dreaming*

Backwards through many modes of being
we have moved into this cool sea-current
where in undifferentiated form
we are the grey-green tide that we inhabit.
At first high in a rocky landscape
we watched or were archaic heroes,
tangled in myth and brittle with tradition,
who followed out the patterns of a quest;
and meeting for the scene of conflict
found all transformed by rippling light.
Then the pulsating union of great cats,
furred and fierce, with grey eyes – our eyes.
The air shifted and grew still;
surf rose from a slow sea,
and plants, set like fleshy stars in the rocks,
read without eyes each other's history.
So the protean pictures passed
and fell away. Now we are water,
or almost water-plankton or protozoa,
adrift in a distant wash of sucking tides.
Still our mythology clings about us;
still we meet and still combine.

IV *Waking*

My eyes open with a click
and meet your eyes, fixed on mine
with a steady gaze that licks at my waking face
patiently, like a gentle tongue, and clinging
as fur to fingers. Even when I blink
I can hear you watching me.

Daylight shouting at the windows
recalls the sky of sun-shot cloud,
the world of times and weather. To which we turn
without reluctance, now. There is no need
for your hand on my breast or your light breath in my hair:
your silent gaze holds me.

Wooing the Muse
(A note for Robert Graves)

In compensation for those painful days
when, pale with lust, we strive with a Medusa
who petrifies each image in the mind,
disarming us of syllable and phrase –
the poet's art is that of the seducer,
and words too often fight him off – we find
rarely, and with gratitude, a moment
when the words flame and fuse, each one revealing
the next, and all arranged in their right places
inevitably; so lovers reach fulfilment
and fall back to gaze stunned at the ceiling,
laughing and weak, as the sweat cools on their faces.

Index

137

'Under the Lawn', 91, 93
'Wren Song', 91
UNCOLLECTED POEMS
'English Childhood,
    My', 110
'Kuaotunu', 9, 35, 110,
'Linseed', 10, 110,
ANTHOLOGIES AND
TRANSLATIONS
Crasnaru, Daniela,
    Letters from Darkness,
    ix, 48
*Faber Book of Twentieth
    Century Women's
    Poetry, The*, xi, 63
*Hugh Primas and the
    Archpoet*, xi, 48, 83
*Oxford Book of
    Contemporary New
    Zealand Poetry, The*, x,
    47
Tartler, Grete, *Orient
    Express*, xi, 48
*Virgin and the
    Nightingale, The*, x, 48
Adcock, Eva (*née* Eggington),
    100–01, 103
Adcock, Irene (Adcock's
    mother), viii, ix, xi, 8, 10,
    11, 13, 17, 19, 37, 42, 43, 46,
    56–7, 98
Adcock, Sam, 100, 103
Ali, Monica, 6
ancestor(s), 2, 5, 6, 7, 13, 14,
    29, 30, 42, 43, 56, 90, 94,
    98–108, 110; ancestral
    (re)connection, 98, 107
Archpoet, The, ix, 48, 83
Auden, W.H., 21

Baxter, James K., ix, 9, 53
Beer, Patricia, 63
Bell, Martin, 27
Bhabha, Homi, 6, 36, 98
Brah, Avtah, 29
Brasch, Charles, x
Bromley, Roger, 48
Brooke, Rupert, 17
Brooks, Martha (*née*
    Hamilton), 42, 99
Brooks, Richey, 42, 99
Brownjohn, Alan, 27–8
Browning, Robert, 17

Campbell, Alistair Te Ariki, ix,
    9, 19, 51, 55
Campbell, Andrew (Adcock's
    son), ix, 1, 19, 23
Campbell, Gregory (Adcock's
    son) , ix, 19, 37, 38
Carter, Angela, 64, 66, 88
Catullus, 21
Childs, Peter, 122
Courage, James, 3
Couzyn, Jeni, 63, 121
Crump, Barry, x, 20

Davin, Dan, 3, 29
Diaspora, diasporic, 3–4, 6, **7**,
    28, 29, 41, 48, 49, 50, 50, 87,
    94, 97, 98, 109; diasporic
    identity, 108; diasporic
    imaginary, 3, 4, 18;
    diasporic subject, 50, 61,
    86, 87, 98
Dowling, Basil, 28
Duckworth, Marilyn
    (Adcock's sister), viii, 1, 10,
    11, 16, 49, 54–5, 56
Duffy, Carol Ann, 62, 64